Lynn Williams is a worksho[...]
She is based in the west of England.

RITUALS
for an Enchanted Life

Simple Steps to Make Your World Wonderful

Lynn Williams

RIDER
LONDON · SYDNEY · AUCKLAND · JOHANNESBURG

1 3 5 7 9 10 8 6 4 2

First published in 2002 by Rider,
an imprint of Ebury Press, Random House,
20 Vauxhall Bridge Road, London SW1V 2SA

Random House Australia (Pty) Limited
20 Alfred Street, Milsons Point, Sydney,
New South Wales 2061, Australia

Random House New Zealand Limited
18 Poland Road, Glenfield,
Auckland 10, New Zealand

Random House South Africa (Pty) Limited
Endulini, 5A Jubilee Road,
Parktown 2193, South Africa

The Random House Group Limited Reg. No. 954009

Papers used by Rider are natural, recyclable products made from wood grown
in sustainable forests.

Printed and bound by MacKays of Chatham plc, Kent

A CIP catalogue record for this book
is available from the British Library

ISBN 0-7126-1591-1

Contents

Introduction

Rituals for an enchanted life

This book is a guide to the use of rituals in everyday life. It introduces the idea of enchanted living – living and working in deep harmony with ourselves, with those around us, and with the tides and rhythms of life. It looks at how you can use rituals to connect spiritually and emotionally to a life that's something more than just getting up, working, eating and sleeping.

Many of us are experiencing a need for something that brings richness and meaning back into our daily routine. Rituals represent powerful tools for both personal transformation and spiritual development. As well as providing a moment of serenity in a busy day, they also encourage reconnection with the people, places and events around us, as well as with our own soul.

At a time when many of us have to follow hectic and often chaotic schedules, rituals bring a sense of calmness and order, and a still point in which to remember ourselves.

This book gives practical ideas about performing rituals and suggests ways of using them in daily life. It includes rituals to suit a range of needs and occasions – from those as ordinary as the morning shower, to those marking important life events. Among the many rituals in this book you'll find ones focused on:

- The home
- Food, meals and celebrations
- The workplace
- Personal growth
- Friends, family and other relationships
- The yearly cycle

These practical and simple rituals can be used by anyone and are easily adapted to suit individual needs and tastes.

Chapter One

Enchanted Living

Living with soul

In this humdrum, cynical world, wouldn't it be nice to find a little enchantment, a little magic?

Many of us are looking for something that makes life more spiritual and fulfilling, seeking ways to connect, just for a moment, with something wonderful. We want life to be more than just the daily grind; we want it to have meaning and purpose. We want it to have enchantment. Rituals can help us achieve this.

The Need for Enchantment

A little magic is vital to our psychological and spiritual health. A life without wonder and mystery is a very dull life, and a dull life is never an entirely fulfilling one. Rituals put back some of the magic and wonder that everyday existence – traffic jams, income tax, supermarket queues and train delays – knocks out of us.

Rituals can help you find personal and spiritual meaning,

and enhance the quality of your life. A simple ritual will soothe your spirit and rebalance your soul, whatever the rest of your day has been like. It gives you the much needed opportunity to simply stop and tune in to a different state of mind. It offers you the chance to express your emotions, understand your feelings, and explore your place in the universe.

In the long term, rituals will bring about profound changes in your life, benefiting your relationships, expanding your self-esteem, increasing your awareness and developing your personal power and insight. But, from the very beginning, rituals allow you to spend some rare, enchanted moments with yourself and, perhaps, with something beyond yourself.

Ritual for calm

Try this simple ritual to clear your mind and soothe your soul.

YOU WILL NEED:

A candle

Go somewhere quiet and light the candle. Take a deep, calm breath and notice the light from the flame forming a golden globe around you. Imagine this warm light flowing into you and gently melting away any stress or negativity. Let the light fill you, from your feet all the way up through your legs, your stomach, your chest, your arms and shoulders, until it fills your head and your face and you glow with luminous grace. Let it fill your thoughts with quiet radiance.

Spend a few minutes enjoying the sensation, then snuff the candle and carry on with your normal life, refreshed and relaxed.

What is a Ritual?

What do you think of when you hear the word 'ritual'? An empty duty performed out of habit or a mind-numbing routine, perhaps? Or a repetitive, laborious task? Or does ritual, on the other hand, breathe clouds of incense and shimmer with mysterious, flickering shadows?

The reality, as usual, is very different from either stereotype. Although in our more casual and spontaneous society we tend to associate rituals with the elaborate ceremonies of the past, with their convoluted rules and regulations and opulent costumes and paraphernalia, the essential purpose of a ritual is simply to focus your spirit. It creates the space, however briefly, to do something we rarely do in today's world – look after our soul.

In this book you'll find rituals that take just minutes to do, and others that take a whole evening. Any ritual is as simple or as complicated as you want it to be. You can use expensive, elaborate trappings, religious artefacts and magical implements; or simple things like flowers, candles and natural stones and shells. Whatever you choose, they're really only there to engage your imagination and focus your spirit on the matter in hand. The only thing that's really important in any ritual is *you*.

Are there any existing rituals in your life?

Do you have any personal traditions, habits or rituals? Do you, for example, unwind in a particular way when you get in from work? Do you like to do certain things regularly and look forward to them – Sunday morning with the papers and coffee, say? How do you feel about them?

How do you celebrate significant events like birthdays and anniversaries? Do you have ways of celebrating outstanding achievements and commemorating important occasions?

Do you or did you have any rituals or ceremonies in your family? What were they based on? Were they based on family customs, cultural tradition, religious beliefs? What do you feel they say about your family and background? How do they relate to the person you are now?

Have the rituals in your life grown naturally out of your needs and beliefs? Are they comfortable, do they still 'fit' you? In effect, do they represent who you truly are?

The purpose of this book is to bring ritual back as a natural and delightful part of everyday life. Even the simplest ritual imparts a spiritual and emotional meaning to the daily routine – creating a moment of calm, allowing your deeper self to connect to a more spiritual, more magical world.

How rituals work

Rituals occupy the interesting borderland between ceremony and spell. They can be powerful tools for self-development and change. Even if a ritual does nothing more than provide a moment of reflection, it can still calm the mind and rebalance the soul. It can energise both the spirit and the will. Rituals give us the opportunity to express our wishes and dreams, to recognise our emotions, and to come to terms with our place in the scheme of things. Most of all, rituals allow us to turn any chosen moment into something special, enhancing the quality of life.

So, how do they work?

They work on the simple idea that by harnessing the power of the imagination you influence your unconscious mind to change the way it sees the world. And by changing the way your unconscious mind sees the world, you change the way you perceive and are perceived by other people, thereby enriching your life, enhancing your self-esteem and lots of other immensely helpful things.

Your unconscious mind finds actions much more inspiring than thoughts. You can, for example, think endlessly about writing that novel; dream about it, fantasise about it, tell yourself that you really are going to do it *one day*. Yet despite all this thinking, somehow you just never get around to it. Why? Because your unconscious mind isn't taking you seriously.

On the other hand, if you buy a stack of paper, draw up a timetable that allows you an hour every day for writing, and make a big 'Do not disturb' notice to hang on your door, your unconscious mind might become more interested. And when it becomes interested, it starts to get things moving.

Suddenly, you'll find writing classes and groups you didn't know existed, you'll come across people and situations who are absolutely begging to be put in a book, you'll meet a writer or someone in publishing and have a really useful conversation with them. When your unconscious mind is interested in what you are doing, it begins to send you inspiration.

Rituals work in just the same way and, if anything, they affect the unconscious even more strongly.

Why? As our understanding of the unconscious mind and the way it communicates improves, this question becomes easier, if not more simple, to answer.

Rituals rely heavily on symbols, and symbols, whether they are actions or objects, are the actual language of the unconscious. They occur in dreams, myths and metaphors, and they speak to us at a far more profound level than our conscious minds can achieve. Rituals use symbolism to reach beyond the rational mind. A unique atmosphere is created which appeals to the powerful intelligence of the unconscious, and actions and objects rich in symbolic meaning are used to encourage it to bring about far-reaching change.

If, for example, you just think about changing some part of your life, your unconscious might not take any notice. It has, literally, heard it all before. But perform a ritual with candles and incense, finishing with the old and welcoming in the new, and you will find your unconscious mind is right there behind

8

you, supporting you every step of the way. And your unconscious is a very powerful ally to have, believe me.

When you want to change, it's essential you do something,
however simple, however symbolic, to excite your unconscious
mind and get it interested.

Ritual for release

Try it for yourself. Think of something in your life you'd be
better off without – a habit, an addiction, a bad relationship, a
negative thought, a limiting belief – and try this ritual.

YOU WILL NEED:

Two white candles

Two pieces of paper and a pen

A fireproof container

A red ribbon or cord

*A symbol of what you want to be rid of. It could be
an actual thing associated with what you want to
be free of – a cigarette, a chocolate bar, a
photograph, a letter, something from an unhappy
past, etc. If what you want to let go of is more
abstract, find a picture (from a magazine, for
example) that represents it – a couple having an
argument, a child looking lonely, an angry face,
etc. If you're totally stuck, draw a rough symbol
yourself – a teardrop for an unhappy*

relationship, a red starburst for an explosive temper. Use your imagination – whatever feels right to you will work

Light the candles. Sit in their quiet light for a while and think about what you want to change. Think about what you want to be rid of, and what you want to have in its place.

Look at the symbol you have chosen. You may want to express your feelings about its effect on your life. If so, talk to it directly, tell it how you feel, just as if you were talking to another person. Take one of the sheets of paper and write down what you want to get rid of, starting, 'I now rid myself of …' or 'I now free myself from …'

Fold your symbol and the sheet of paper together (or wrap one in the other, if that's more manageable). Light them in one of the candle flames and drop them into the fireproof container. Say a heart-felt goodbye and watch until they burn to ash.

Take the other sheet of paper and write down what you want instead – good health, happiness, a loving relationship, self-worth, etc. Start with, 'I now have …' or 'I am now …'. Take a moment to imagine your future and take pleasure in it. Roll the paper up and tie it with the red ribbon or cord and hold it up to the candle flame to bless it. Snuff out the candles and put the rolled paper somewhere you will see it often. Watch what changes.

A bridge between the worlds

A ritual builds a bridge between the inner world and the outer one. It links the body, mind and soul indivisibly so that all three work together for effective change. Most importantly, it takes your thoughts and turns them into something physical and real. Thoughts just stay in your head; rituals take place in the real world – you can see, hear, feel, smell and even, sometimes, taste what's going on.

For the same reason, it's useful to write down goals and intentions so that they are in the real world rather than just in your own head. Write down wishes, write down your hopes and dreams. You don't have to show them to anyone if you don't want to, they are there to make your wishes real to you and your unconscious mind.

Making life magical

Through ritual, we can tap into the enormous power of the human imagination. A commitment made in casual conversation, however sincere, cannot compare with one made in a ritual where the unconscious mind, the will and the reason all work in unison.

And, who knows, the help of a higher self or higher powers might also be invoked – symbolic guardians and helpers who inspire magical results. If this is so, then all things become possible.

Make the rituals your own

It's very unlikely that you will do all the rituals in this book, starting at page one and going right through them to the end. It's more likely that you'll pick out one or two that instantly appeal to you, earmark some others to come back to, and skip those that don't seem relevant. Before you even bought the book, you probably flicked through it and found that one or two things caught your eye. You've already started to make these rituals your own.

Rituals can be simple or complex. This book suggests various traditional things such as candles, flowers, crystals and natural objects to focus the mind. But if something in particular works for you – a particular form of religious symbolism or spiritual belief, say – then by all means, use it. There is nothing fixed or rigid about these rituals. Remember, at its most simple, a ritual needs nothing more than a quiet moment and a reason for doing it.

Use the ideas here as inspiration, as recommendations rather than inflexible rules. Follow your intuition. A good ritual should touch your soul and leave you feeling uplifted. If anything irritates, grates or feels uncomfortable about the ritual, then change it. If you feel something is missing, add it. Make these your rituals; alter and adapt them to suit *you*.

If you want to do something that isn't covered in this book, then you can plan your own rituals. Either start with something that comes close to what you want and adapt it, or start from scratch – most of the longer rituals in this book follow a simple four-stage plan:

- Energise – do something, such as lighting a candle, which sets the time and place aside as something special
- Connect – symbolically link your unconscious mind to the reason for the ritual
- Perform the ritual
- Complete the ritual by either letting go of an unwanted object or binding a desirable one

Have fun!

Rituals exist for you, not you for rituals. Don't ever fall into the trap of thinking you *have* to do a ritual for any reason. They should never be boring or something you think of as an obligation – 'I *have* to do a ritual bath this evening.' ' It's Beltane, I *must* celebrate it.' 'It's the new moon, I *really should* do a ritual.' Rituals are there to make the ordinary magical, not make the ordinary even more mind-numbingly tedious by loading you up with extra chores.

Learn from children. They know exactly how to do rituals, only most of the time they call it playing. We come into the world with an inherent awareness of the magical and an under-standing of the enchanted life.

As children, we learned about the world almost entirely through play. We learned who we were and how and where we fitted into the great scheme of things purely through acting out the ideas and fantasies in our heads. We opened up all the possibilities of life and tried them all out, regardless of whether they were sensible, realistic or practical.

Unhappily, for many of us these expeditions into the realms of the imagination were gradually forgotten as we grew up. But even as adults it is still possible to rediscover the value of a playful imagination through ritual and find again that sacred realm, the place of creativity, dreams and imagination, and rediscover the magic in life.

Rituals will give you the opportunity to rediscover both your sense of wonder and your sense of fun. Given the chance, they'll also empower you and encourage you to expand and enrich your life and reach your full potential. Rituals enhance your life and encourage you to explore it more fully. They empower, support and comfort you. Above all, they help you rediscover a sense of enchantment and the pure magic of being alive.

All in all, they add enormously to the sheer joy of existence. And when you find you enjoy your favourite rituals so much they've simply become part of your everyday routine, you'll know you're getting close to an enchanted life.

Doing Rituals

Most rituals are very simple and straightforward and different ones for different purposes are fully explained in their own chapters. There are, though, two fundamental skills you will need. They're described here in detail, but they're not actually very complicated. When you read them you'll probably find they are things you know how to do already. Most people understand and use them instinctively. They are:

- Intention, and
- Visualisation

Intention

A clear intention gives you focus, and when you are focused you can achieve almost anything.

- Work out clearly what you want to achieve – feel peaceful, overcome an obstacle, release yourself from something, feel energised ... whatever you like
- Get a clear picture of it in your own mind
- Imagine moving that picture down into your heart so that you feel it as well as see it
- Vividly imagine power pouring into you, into your heart and into the image that you hold there. Feel the power filling you with a sense of positivity. The power can be anything you feel is right for you – clear white light, universal love, spiritual energy, anything
- When you feel that clearly, you are ready to begin

Visualisation

Visualisation is the key that lends your personal power to the ritual. It unlocks the powerful energy within you that connects you to the universe.

- Sit quietly and close your eyes
- Take three deep, slow, calming breaths
- If you've been asked to visualise a clear, golden light filling your body, for example, concentrate and imagine light filling your head as if you were almost breathing it in with each breath
- Imagine the light flowing into your heart and spreading out, filling your whole body
- Feel the light illuminating you from within
- Sense the light streaming into you and vividly imagine it flooding your whole body until you are immersed in a sea of light
- Hold this image for a few minutes. If your thoughts wander away from it, draw them gently back
- Always ground yourself after visualisation and before doing anything that demands practical concentration such as driving a car or operating machinery. Walk around, stamp your feet, stretch, have something to eat and drink

Health and Safety

Rituals are not generally hazardous, but one or two points should be kept in mind.

Candles

- Always use a candlestick or holder designed for the

purpose. This is especially important when using candles on the floor where they can be knocked over more easily
- Never leave candles unattended
- Take care using flammable materials such as dried herbs, ribbons and paper
- Make sure candles are snuffed out after use

Herbs and essential oils
- Herbs and oils used in this book are not intended for internal use
- Take care handling herbs and oils if you are pregnant. If in doubt, check with your GP or a qualified herbalist or aromatherapist
- The same applies if you have skin disorders, epilepsy, or any condition you feel gives reason for caution

Incense
- Burn incense sticks in an appropriate holder and don't leave them unattended
- Make sure there is sufficient ventilation
- If you are using the sort of incense that is burned on charcoal blocks, buy the blocks from a reputable supplier and follow the instructions on the packet
- Charcoal and incense can smoulder for a long time. Always burn them in a heatproof container, and don't leave this on a surface that may be damaged by heat. Make sure the charcoal is thoroughly cold before disposing of the ashes

Finally

This book provides an introduction to using rituals. It gives you ideas to try out – ideas about doing things and visualising things, and about making altars and using them. It gives advice about everyday rituals you can use to bring a spiritual element into just about everything from your morning shower to your evening meal. The most important element, though, is you.

Enjoy using these rituals; experiment and find out what works best for you. As you continue to work with spiritual energy you will become increasingly connected to the universe, and your intuition and sensitivity will develop accordingly. It is then that you will start to build an enchanted existence for yourself, and for your family and friends within the magic circle of your own life.

Chapter Two

Everyday Rituals

Magical moments
for every day

Enchanted living sounds like a wonderful idea, but where on earth do you find the time for enchantment in your everyday life? For most of us, the timetable's packed tight enough with life's practicalities without having to make space for the magical as well.

Don't despair. This chapter looks at the very simplest rituals, ones you can slot almost unnoticed into your daily life. They take moments to do, but uplift you and enliven your day just as effectively as those that take hours.

A charmed life

Wouldn't it be terrific to wake up every morning feeling refreshed and inspired, fully connected to the day ahead?

Rather than trudging through the same old routine day after

day, wouldn't it be nice if you could start your morning with enthusiasm and energy, top up your vitality throughout the day and let go of all your stress at the end of it?

Nothing is too ordinary, too basic or so mundane it can't be made a whole lot more interesting and significant with the aid of a ritual or two. And the best rituals are those that are so simple and so enjoyable they simply become part of your daily schedule.

You don't have to do each and every one of them. As you read through, one or two will catch your fancy – try those first. As you try them, see what sticks and what feels like it could make a difference for you.

Good Mornings

When you wake up, take a few moments to fully arrive in the day.

Wake up and breathe

Breath is the essence of life. How we feel – invigorated or exhausted, refreshed or depressed – often depends on our breathing. When we are tense our breathing automatically becomes shallow and constricted, as if we fear letting go. Our energy becomes restricted, we get more tense, and breathing becomes even more shallow. A couple of good deep breaths breaks that cycle and restores normality.

Reconnect with your body first thing and wake up, literally, to the present moment.

YOU WILL NEED:

Just you

Take long, calm, gentle breaths in through your nose and out through your mouth. Visualise breathing in warm, joyful, morning light with each breath, drawing it deep into your body. Feel it diffusing gradually throughout every part of you, spreading a feeling of vitality and wellbeing as it does.

Next, breathe the day awake. As you breathe in, visualise breathing in the day ahead. Imagine drawing it into you and embracing it, committing to it. As you breathe out, let go of the past and any negative experiences, beliefs or limitations.

Open to the day

Try this little ritual to ensure whole-heartedness and passion for the day ahead.

YOU WILL NEED:

A window, preferably the one with the most attractive (or least unattractive) view

Stand at the window, looking out at the world. Focus your thoughts on the region of your heart and feel this area becoming relaxed and warm. Visualise a vibrant green light, like the sun seen through leaves, growing from a point within your heart and expanding until it shimmers throughout your chest.

Open your arms and imagine holding the day you see before you in your arms and drawing it into your heart. Feel your heart open up to receive it. Say 'Yes', *and mean it*.

If it's a particularly bright, sunny day with a blue sky, open your arms to the sky as well and draw it into your heart. Breathe in the colour and feel it tingling right through your body. Let your mind and thoughts fill with soft blue brightness.

Mirror, mirror

This has to be the simplest ritual ever.

YOU WILL NEED:

A mirror

First thing in the morning, look in the mirror and smile. It doesn't even have to be a real smile; a false one works just as well. Think of all the things a smile symbolises – friendship, approval, joy, welcome, encouragement … Look in the mirror and smile every morning – the lift it gives you outshines Prozac any day.

Power shower

Use your morning shower to cleanse your mind and spirit as well as your body.

YOU WILL NEED:

Shower

Salt

As you step under the shower, imagine you are standing in a crystal-clear pool under a beautiful waterfall in a flower-filled garden. Let the water wash over you, dissolving and washing away any negativity within you. Feel any doubts, fears or resentments within you just melting away.

Take a handful of salt and rub it lightly over your body. Salt is a natural purifier, both physically and spiritually. As you rinse it off, imagine sunlight pouring down, mingling with the water and filling you with radiance.

Power dressing

Use getting dressed in the morning as an opportunity to put on positive energies along with your clothes. Dressing can have strong ritual significance in itself. Think of a priest donning vestments, judges robing up, a bride dressing for her wedding, or even just the feeling of rising anticipation while getting dressed for a party.

YOU WILL NEED:

The clothes you intend to wear

Lay out the clothes you intend to wear. Touch each one in turn and sense it becoming charged with a positive quality of your choosing. You might, for example, invest your shoes with determination as you see them walking purposefully down your chosen path. You might want a petticoat to embody feminine qualities, or a jumper to personify playfulness. You might decide a tie should symbolise benign authority. Dress with concentration and purpose and, as you put on each garment, feel those qualities clothing you.

Choose the colour of your clothing to suit your needs for the day ahead. You don't have to dress all in one colour; a blouse or shirt, scarf or tie will add the necessary spark. Try:

RED when you need courage and confidence

ORANGE when you need energy and spontaneity

YELLOW for optimism and a clear mind

GREEN to combat stress and remain balanced

TURQUOISE to resist adverse influences

BLUE when you need to express yourself clearly and with calm authority

PINK when you want to appear approachable and unthreatening

VIOLET when you are feeling spiritual

Blow away blues

When you have the morning blues, this is an excellent way to get rid of them.

YOU WILL NEED:

Feathers

A piece of blue ribbon

A few hairs from your head

A place out of doors – or an open window if this isn't possible

Tie the feathers and some of your hairs into a bunch with the ribbon. Hang them up outside somewhere where they'll catch the wind. As they blow around in the breeze, feel your blues wafting away.

Here are a couple of 'card tricks' to lift your spirits and inspire your soul each morning. Once you've made the cards, nothing could be simpler or easier.

Pick a card

YOU WILL NEED:

A pack of small filing cards or blank postcards

Coloured pens and pencils

Photographs cut from magazines

Take the blank cards and write one quality you admire and desire on each one. You might choose things like:

Enthusiasm	Compassion
Warmth	Joy
Spontaneity	Peace
Inspiration	Radiance
Openness	Grace
Courage	Power
Harmony	Playfulness
Creativity	Focus
Freedom	Gentleness
Balance	Commitment
Integrity	Delight

Decorate the cards if you like. You could use pictures to illustrate each word, anything that brings it vividly alive for you. Each morning pick a card and prop it up where you can see it. Either pick one you feel drawn to that day, one with a quality you know you'll need, or just shuffle the pack and choose at random.

Pick a colour

We all respond to colour, consciously or unconsciously, we just can't help it. Every colour delivers a unique message straight to the brain that affects our state of mind. Why not make use of this and make a pack of colour cards to enhance your morning mood.

YOU WILL NEED:

Seven or eight small filing cards or blank postcards

Paints or coloured paper (colour samples from paint charts can be useful)

Photographs cut from magazines

Take the blank cards and cover each of them with a collage of colour using paint, paper and pictures – one colour for each card:

RED is physically stimulating and enlivening; good for boosting energy and drive

ORANGE promotes cheerfulness and a sense of security

YELLOW increases mental activity and encourages optimism

GREEN is restful and balancing

BLUE is calming

PINK promotes happiness and good feelings

PURPLE induces calmness, seriousness and concentration

You could also use an eighth colour – white – for when you simply want to clear and neutralise your mind.

Each morning pick a card and gaze at it for a couple of minutes until you feel saturated with your chosen colour for that day. Keep your colour pack handy for when you need a quick pick-me-up.

Elemental power 1

Wouldn't it be great to have the power of the four elements at your disposal all day long? Make this talisman on a morning when you have the time to do so and wear it every day thereafter. Re-charge it by repeating the ritual when you get the chance.

YOU WILL NEED:

A white candle

Something you can wear or carry with you – a piece of jewellery would be ideal (I have a bracelet made of four strands of beads – turquoise for water, blue for air, green for earth and gold for fire)

Four pictures representing the four elements – ones cut from magazines would do

EARTH – picture of a forest, meadow or similar

WATER – picture of sea, lake or stream

FIRE – picture of flames, volcano, etc

AIR – picture of clouds, birds or butterflies

Light the candle and set the four pictures out in front of you. Pass your chosen object over each picture in turn. As you pause over each one, visualise the power of that element pouring into the object, surging through it and into your body.

- Water symbolises cleansing and healing. Visualise it flowing over and through you, washing away all negativity

- Earth is connected with nurturing. Imagine strong roots growing deep into the ground connecting you to the power of life

- Air is symbolic of inspiration. Imagine a cool, fresh breeze blowing all your mental cobwebs away

- Fire represents energy. Feel yourself becoming energised and alive

Lastly, hold your chosen object to your heart and sense yourself perfectly balanced at the centre of the four elements.

Put your talisman on every morning. Touch it or look at it during the day to remind yourself of your elemental power. If you need a little more of one of the elements in your life – more passion or energy, perhaps, or a greater sense of being firmly grounded – put the appropriate picture where you'll see it frequently during the day.

Elemental Power 2

As well as using your element talisman in the morning, make use of the symbolic powers of the elements as and when you need them during the day.

- Fire is energising. When you need extra oomph, strike a match and focus on the flame, absorbing its energy

- Earth is nurturing. When you need a little kindness and encouragement for yourself, stroke the leaves of a plant or touch a flower. Absorb its deep, calm essence
- Water is cleansing. Wash your hands when you wish to rid yourself of something negative
- Air is inspiring. Take a deep breath and let it out slowly when you need to clear your mind

Good Days

However good your start to the day, things almost invariably crop up. Keep your soul clear throughout the day with these simple rituals. Look through them and choose the ones that appeal to you.

Grounding

Stress can make you feel detached and scattered – 'absent' from your body. Being firmly present in your physical body feels much more comfortable and enables you to stay in control and deal with things much more calmly and easily. Try these methods for grounding yourself.

- Deliberately stretch and yawn. Even if you start by just pretending to do it, I can guarantee you'll end up doing it for real
- Breathe out. Stressed breathing is shallow and high in the chest. Deepen your breathing by exhaling fully, expelling all

the air from your lungs before letting the next breath flow in naturally

- Stamp on the ground. If you are on solid ground, outdoors for preference, stamp hard two or three times and experience the earth solidly beneath your feet

- Keep a stone somewhere handy for just these moments. Hold it in your hands, feel the shape and weight of it. Think about the deep earth or deep sea it came from

- Sit down and focus your attention on the base of your spine. Imagine strong roots growing out of you and going deep down into the earth. Concentrate on getting those roots really deep and firmly anchored

Releasing

Sometimes, conversely, instead of grounding you need releasing. When you feel heavy and stuck, try these methods to get your soul flying again.

- As you breathe deeply and calmly, imagine the air in your lungs turning into a fountain of light, welling up and cascading out through the top of your head

- If it's breezy, stand by an open window or door. Feel the wind and imagine it gently blowing through you, blowing all the cobwebs away

- Pleat a fan out of yellow paper. Keep your eyes on it as you pleat and thoroughly absorb that yellow. Fan your face, your head and the back of your neck with it

- Look up into the sky (being careful not to look into the sun, of course). Let your mind follow your gaze higher and higher into the blue

Quick cleansers

Sometimes you just need something quick and easy to refresh your spirit or your environment during the day.

- Ring a bell – find one with a sweet, clear tone
- Keep fresh flowers or plants near you and take odd moments during the day just to gaze at their colour until you feel fully saturated with it
- Keep a fresh growing herb in a pot. Every so often, close your eyes, brush your hands over the leaves and breathe in their scent
- Close your eyes and visualise yourself sitting under a rainbow. Let the rainbow descend and gently enclose your whole body in an aura of rainbow light
- Do an elemental cleansing: breathe out deeply to expel the staleness from your body and blow out bad thoughts. Splash your face with water to wash away negativity. Take a pinch of salt and press it to your forehead, heart and solar plexus to purify and ground you. Strike a match or light a candle to burn away impurities and recharge your energy

Decisions, decisions

Take the drudgery out of decision-making. Once you've made the cards, using them is simple and easy. You don't have to agree with what the card says, but how you react to the decision might clarify how you feel about things.

YOU WILL NEED:

A pack of small filing cards or blank postcards

Coloured pens and pencils

Take the blank cards and write on each one a possible answer to the sort of problems you encounter. You could put things like:

- Yes
- No
- Wait
- Ask someone you trust
- Do nothing yet
- Get more information
- Do something new
- Consider what you did last time this happened
- Think what Wonder Woman/Superman would do
- Visit somewhere nice for inspiration
- Ask an expert
- Ask the opinion of three other people
- Take the option you like least

- Take the option you like most
- Sleep on it
- Ask a stranger about it

Decorate the cards if you like. You could use pictures to illustrate the solution where appropriate.

When you need to make a decision but can't make up your mind, shuffle the cards and pick one out at random. Think about how the chosen solution might answer the problem and how you feel about it.

Magical doorways

Doors can be highly symbolic things. Make ritual use of the doorways around your house and at work to energise both you and your environment on a regular basis. Give a particular door special symbolic value for use in a number of ways.

YOU WILL NEED:

A doorway

A key

A spray mister – plant spray or empty perfume spray bottle – filled with rosewater or any other scented water

The door can be an internal one or one leading to the outside, whatever feels right to you. Open the door and spray the space thoroughly with the scented water. Use your imagination to see a 'door' of mist and water there in the

opening. Visualise it shimmering with light and possibilities.
Use your magical door for making changes:

- Every time you pass through it imagine any negativity within you being trapped, held and dissolved away in the watery mist

- When you want to make changes within yourself or your life, open the door and imagine the wished-for state lies on the other side. Step through the door into your desire

- When you need more of a sense of abundance and plenty in your life, open the door and visualise good things pouring in through it

- If you need to get rid of a bad atmosphere – after a quarrel or disagreement, perhaps – sweep all the bad feelings out through the door and imagine them being dissolved away as they pass through the mist

- Bad thoughts, feelings, memories and even bad dreams can be vigorously swept out through the door as well

- For yet another use, see *Step into the positive* below

Step into the positive

You can literally step into a more positive frame of mind. The more often you do it, the more powerful it becomes.

YOU WILL NEED:

A definite place marked out on the floor

There are various possible ways to mark out your magic spot; you could use the pattern on the floor, mark out a place with chalk, string or pebbles, use two sides of a doorway, or whatever else you think of.

Stand on the marked place and remember a time when you felt really strong and positive. Remember as fully and as clearly as you can – recapture all the sights and sounds and, especially, the feelings. Walk away from the spot and rest for a few minutes. Stand in place again and remember again, adding more details if you can and intensifying all the positive feelings you experience as you do so.

Move away again and rest for a few moments. This time, when you step firmly back into the marked space you should automatically feel those good feelings – you will be literally stepping into your positive self. Do this a few times, recapturing the positive experience each time.

Your unconscious mind should now associate a determined step forward with that positive experience. Try it out a few times to see if you recapture those good feelings just by stepping forward and stepping into your positive self. For the next couple of days you should be able to feel strong and positive just by taking a determined step forward. When it begins to wear off, just repeat the ritual to 'recharge' it.

Running free

Use exercise sessions to tone up your spirit as well as your body. Visualise actively releasing negativity as you work.

- Outrun problems as you jog

- Stamp on negative thoughts in the step class

- Drown your sorrows at the swimming pool

- Override all obstacles on your mountain bike

- Get to grips with burdens with the same determination you use to lift weights

Turn physical energy into emotional energy and power your way through problems. Use your imagination to visualise how your particular form of exercise could be used to ban the blues.

Come to your senses

Take a few moments in a busy day literally to come to your senses and remember who, what and where you are.

- SIGHT – Look up and relax your gaze. What do you see ahead of you? Notice the colours and the light. Without moving your eyes, what can you see at the edges of your field of vision? Don't forget above and below as well as left and right

- SOUND – What do you hear? What can you hear behind that sound, even further away? What's the most distant thing you hear?

- SMELL – Breathe in quietly, what can you smell?

- TASTE – What can you taste? Anything?
- FEELING – How does your body feel at this moment? Does it feel relaxed and balanced? Gently adjust your posture, if necessary, until you feel poised and comfortable

Take a deep breath and feel right at the centre of all your senses for a moment before you carry on with whatever you were doing.

Picture peace

YOU WILL NEED:

An appealing landscape from a book or magazine

Card for mounting

Next time you see a picture of a beautiful peaceful scene in which you feel you could relax, cut it out or photocopy it and keep it.

When you feel frazzled, just gaze at your picture – beach, forest, mountain meadow, whatever. Imagine yourself there and add details such as sounds and scents to make it feel even more real. Imagine where you are seeing the scene from – a cosy cabin? A castle? Pick somewhere you would feel comfortable and relaxed.

Think of your picture as the doorway to a five-minute holiday you can take whenever you like. Collect a range of pictures you can use to match your moods and fantasies.

Soul book

Make something to dip into to cheer yourself up when you need it.

YOU WILL NEED:

A scrapbook or blank notebook

Pens and pencils

Pictures, cuttings, postcards, etc

Feathers, ribbons, sequins, beads

Start collecting things that make you smile. They can be funny or touching:

- Letters from friends
- Postcards
- Photographs of happy times
- Jokes
- Cartoons
- Inspiring quotes
- Uplifting pictures
- Poems
- Limericks
- Children's drawings
- Tickets, menus, mementoes

Stick them into the book and decorate the pages with ribbons, beads, whatever you like. Open the book at random whenever you need a bit of a lift.

Dish the dirt

Did you know washing dishes could be a spiritual, soul-expanding experience? No, I took some convincing too, but try this tiny everyday ritual for yourself and see what happens.

YOU WILL NEED:

Dirty dishes

Rubber gloves

Hot, soapy water

It's important to have plenty of hot water and washing-up liquid so the water stays hot and foamy rather than tepid and scummy. Replace the water with fresh water whenever necessary. Rubber gloves are important too so you can plunge your hands right in and still feel protected. (With rubber gloves you can do anything – you are invincible.)

Imagine the dirty dishes are your problems, obstacles, hang-ups and worries. As you wash them, visualise washing away all your negativity. Attack them with vigour. Everything will come out sparkling fresh, bright and shining clean. Believe your unconscious mind will attack your problems with the same energy and with the same result.

Good Nights

Lots of people have bedtime rituals; little routines that let their body and subconscious mind know it's time to close down for the night. Interestingly, it's been found those who do tend to get a better night's sleep and wake up more refreshed than those who don't.

The best plan for a restful night seems to be:

- Go to bed at a regular time
- Have a warm, relaxing bath first
- Drink herbal teas with a relaxing effect (camomile, for example) in the late evening, rather than tea or coffee
- Keep your bedroom just for relaxing in rather than working, watching television, etc

All these elements can become part of your own personal night-time ritual.

Soul bath

Wash away the day from your body and your soul with this extra-deep cleansing bath.

YOU WILL NEED:

Warm bath

Candles

Salt

Herbs or flowers – see suggestions below

Piece of fabric – a handkerchief or scarf would be fine

Rubber band

Oats or oatmeal

Make a herb-bundle to go in the bath. Put a tablespoon of oatmeal in the centre of the fabric and add around a teaspoon to a tablespoon the herbs or flowers of your choosing. Gather up the fabric and secure the top with the rubber band.

The following are some suggestions for flowers or herbs you could use. (Please check the suitability of all herbs and oils if you are pregnant or breastfeeding, or tend to suffer from allergic reactions.)

ROSE PETALS – for love, beauty and a gentle soul

PANSIES (heartsease) – to calm stressful thoughts and worries

LAVENDER – for relaxation

CAMOMILE – to aid good sleep

MINT – for strength and health

ORANGE PEEL – for joy and laughter

ROSEMARY – when you want to be alert and refreshed for the evening ahead

ALLSPICE – for playfulness and creativity

JUNIPER – when you need to cleanse deep negativity

Arrange the candles round the bath and light them. Drop a handful of salt into the water – salt is a great purifier, cleansing both body and spirit.

Put the herb-bundle in the bath and watch the water turn milky and mysterious. Relax in the water as you visualise it gently drawing out all the stresses and strains of the day and replacing them with positive thoughts and feelings.

Power undressing

As you shed your clothes, visualise shedding all the day's irritations, problems, niggles and worries along with them.

Serenity candle

When you can't switch off in the evenings, there's nothing like a quiet spell of candlelight for calming the mind.

YOU WILL NEED:

A blue candle

A toothpick, pin or something similar

A cup of camomile tea

Inscribe the rune Lagu Ⲅ on the candle with the toothpick. Lagu is the rune of attunement and harmony. Its meaning is water and it symbolises the ebb and flow of life.

Light the candle and enjoy its quiet light for ten minutes or so while you sip your camomile tea.

Candlelight angels

Take some quiet moments at the end of the day to reflect and dream by candlelight.

YOU WILL NEED:

Blue candle

Pen and paper

Light the candle and think back over the day. Pick out the three best things that have happened, however small they may be, and take time to really appreciate them.

If you wish, while you have a candle lit, write a short prayer giving thanks for the day just gone and asking for luck and happiness for the next. Slip it under the candle and imagine the light of the candle beaming your prayer to the universe.

Forgive and forget

If the events of the day still niggle, try this gentle visualisation to help you let go of them.

Close your eyes and breathe slowly and calmly. Imagine you are walking through a beautiful garden filled with flowers. Ahead of you a fountain of rainbow light leaps and plays in the sunshine. Step into the fountain and let the light cascade over you. Feel the colours streaming through you, washing away all the bad stuff. As you do so, say to yourself, 'I forgive and let go'. Let the colours just dissolve the negativity and carry it all away.

When you are ready, retrace your steps through the garden and gently return to normal.

Guardian angels

Focus on positive images and beneficial thoughts to help settle your mind and prepare you for deep, restful, healing sleep.

If you would like to feel protected while you're sleeping, call on a little angelic guardianship to help you feel safe and secure.

YOU WILL NEED:

Just your imagination

As you lie in bed, breathe gently and imagine a warm, golden light growing in your heart. Visualise this light growing and expanding outwards until it fills the whole room.

Call the four Archangels – they symbolise ancient and powerful forces of protection and healing. Focus on each one in turn and let their specific qualities flow around you and into you.

MICHAEL – stands at your head with a golden sword and armour to protect you

RAPHAEL – stands at your feet to ease your tensions and bring healing and peace

GABRIEL – stands on your right and brings a strong and courageous heart

URIEL – stands on your left and brings wisdom and understanding

Chapter Three

The Enchanted Home

Sanctuary for your soul

You know when you're in a home with soul, you can feel it in your bones. You feel relaxed yet uplifted. Your roots feel nourished and your spirit can blossom. A home with soul gives you four great treasures:

- A feeling of belonging
- Rest for your body
- Harmony for mind and spirit
- Sustenance for your heart

Every home, ideally, should be a sanctuary for the body, mind and soul. It should be a place of comfort and renewal where you can recharge your spiritual batteries in peace and harmony. It should also be a place for creativity and play, somewhere where you can be your true self and explore your full potential.

This chapter looks at ways to achieve this desirable state. One way is by clearing away unwanted negative energy and replacing it with positive blessings. Another way is to dedicate space for the things you want to happen.

Sanctuary

How do you create the right atmosphere in your home? As you begin to make rituals and blessings a part of your daily life, the mood of your home will naturally change, becoming more creative and fulfilling. But before we get on to spiritual matters, ask yourself some basic questions about where you live. Do you have a home where you feel at home?

- What effect does colour have on you? Would using more colour, less colour or a different colour in your home change your energy or mood?

    RED is warm and uplifting, giving you courage and confidence

    ORANGE is stimulating and cheerful, increasing energy and spontaneity

    YELLOW is the colour of sunshine, encouraging optimism and a clear mind

    GREEN is natural and harmonious, suggesting relaxation and balance

    TURQUOISE is emotionally supportive, suggesting the sea

    BLUE is peaceful, cooling and calm

    PINK is gentle and cheerful when pale, vibrant when strong

VIOLET is very soothing, becoming more
mysterious as the colour deepens

- Do you need to add light and space to your home?
  Lighting, colour, mirrors and simpler window
  treatments make a profound difference
- Conversely, does it feel too Spartan or exposed?
  Curtains, screens and dividers could be the answer
- Does where you live express who and what you are?
  Are there places for you to do what you want to do? Are
  you surrounded by things you love?
- Do you need to clear out clutter?
- Are you hanging on to things that have unhappy
  memories for you?
- Is everything chosen and loved by you?

Your Soul Home

Your soul home is the place where you feel relaxed and at
peace. If you feel home is just the place you hang your hat,
make your home more conducive to spiritual harmony with
these rituals. They'll help you understand what you need and
what your home needs.

Easy chair

Make a special place just for you. A chair, a sofa or even a floor-cushion where you just sit and relax.

Make it your own. Cover it with fabric you like, arrange tables, lights and whatever else you need for your comfort. Make sure you can see something attractive from it – a pleasant view, a bowl of flowers or a picture, for example.

The more you use it for relaxation, meditation or simply daydreaming, the more deeply you will associate it with a pleasant sense of peace and tranquillity, and the easier it will be for you to fall into that relaxed state just by sitting there.

Picture this – happy home

This ritual helps you feel more connected to your home. It will help you focus on what your home means to you and clarify what you want out of it. It also activates your unconscious mind to set about actually getting it for you.

YOU WILL NEED:

Two candles

Large sheet of paper or card

A photograph of your family (make sure you're in it, too) – or yourself if you live alone. Include photos of friends and relatives who visit regularly

Pictures that symbolise the things you want to happen in your home – people having fun,

*hugging, entertaining, relaxing, whatever. Cut
them from brochures, magazines, etc. Take your
time choosing, you don't have to complete this
all in one go if you don't want to*

Gold pen and paper

Glue

Light the candles to remind your unconscious you are doing
something special. Take your time and enjoy 'playing'. Glue
the pictures and photos onto the card to make a pleasing
collage. Spend some time contemplating the picture you've
made. Concentrate on the positive impression it presents, and
adjust the image until it feels just right. If you believe
something specific is missing from your home life, include lots
of pictures of it in your collage.

Write the address of your house and the names of the people
living there on the gold paper and paste it on. Put the
photograph of yourself and/or your family right in the very
centre and place the finished collage where you will see it
every day.

Picture this—new home

When you're looking for a new home, sort out what you really dream about and get your unconscious mind working for you with this simple but powerful ritual.

YOU WILL NEED:

The same things as above but with pictures that sum up what you want in your new home – country cottage, smart town house, a wild garden, sea views, swimming pool, vegetable garden, balconies, friendly neighbours, whatever

Light the candle and make up your collage as above. Gaze at the picture you have made and let yourself enter into it. Imagine being in that house. See the things that will give you happiness, hear pleasant sounds around you, and most of all experience the pleasure and satisfaction you will feel there.

Let the candle burn down as you thoroughly enjoy your perfect home. Keep bringing your attention back to the picture and experience that sense of certainty and success. Let the conviction grow inside you that it is waiting for you somewhere out there.

Write your name and those of the other people who will be living in the house with you on the paper and paste it on. Put your family photograph in the middle. Put the collage where you will see it every day and get on with the practical steps towards finding your dream home.

Your home's soul

Do you feel your home has a spirit – an atmosphere and a personality all its own? If you don't, now is the time to give it one. If you do, attuning to it will not only help you listen to what your house wants and needs, it will also help align your soul with your home so you feel truly at ease there.

Honouring your home's soul and providing it with a sanctuary will help you focus on the spiritual essence of where you live, and help harmony flow more easily.

YOU WILL NEED:

Silver candle

A spirit house – use a ready-made doll's house or birdhouse, or make your own little house-shaped box

Flowers, ribbons and anything else you would like to decorate the spirit house with

Sit where you feel the heart of your home is. Light the candle and state your intention – to attune to the spirit of your home.

Visualise a pure silvery light radiating out from the candle and filling the whole house. Picture everything being filled with a soft, translucent light. Breathe in this light. Visualise it penetrating deeply into your mind, illuminating and clarifying your thoughts. Sense it stimulating your intuition, opening up new areas of perception and awareness.

Ask the spirit of your home to be with you. Sit very still and begin to be aware of your surroundings. Attune first to the physical sensations – temperature, scent, sound and vibration. Continue to deepen this awareness. Notice the fainter impressions that come to you and let them guide you even deeper until you feel connected to the soul of your home.

Imagine you can communicate directly with your house's spirit: ask its name, how it would like to be seen or thought of, what it wishes for the house. Notice any feelings, impressions or ideas you get. Let them build a picture in your mind.

Ask the spirit of your house to watch over your home and keep it safe and happy. Decorate the spirit house with flowers and ribbons and anything else you like, inviting the spirit to make its home there. Visualise the silvery light coming to rest on the spirit house, filling it with a soft radiance.

Put your spirit house somewhere in the heart of your home and visit it frequently to light a candle or incense and decorate it with fresh flowers to remind you of that feeling of connection.

Change the Mood

You can change the mood in your home and lighten and brighten the atmosphere very easily. Stagnant, stale and heavy energies accumulate in just the same way stale tobacco smoke lingers in a room after a party or dust and cobwebs collect in an unused one. Energy cleansing is simply the spiritual equivalent of a good spring-clean, sweeping away psychic dust and dirt.

Negative energy can be caused by:

- Stressed family members
- Family arguments and disputes
- Unexpressed undercurrents such as resentment, boredom, anxiety, etc
- Illness
- Stressful or distressing events in the home
- Distressing news or events brought into the home via TV, radio, Internet, newspapers, etc
- Negative emotions such as disappointment, resentment, anger, apathy, etc

A room cleared of negative energy will:

- Look brighter – lighter and cleaner, the colours sharper
- Sound clearer – less muffled and dull than a room with stagnant energy
- Smell fresher – the air clearer and easier to breathe
- Feel lighter – less heavy and oppressive than a negatively charged room

Quick mood changes

There are a number of quick-fix spring cleansers that will brighten things up spiritually:

- Ring a bell
- Get a chiming clock – it will clear the air for you every hour on the hour. Why do you think old houses with grandfather clocks are so mellow and calm?
- Spray the room with scented water from a plant mister

- Open all the windows and doors for a few minutes
- Hang a prism (faceted crystal) in the window to fill the room with darting rainbows
- Play up-beat, lively music
- Conversely, play calming, soothing music if that's what's needed
- Light some incense to increase the spiritual quality of the room
- Light one or more candles
- On a sunny day, clean your windows with energy and inviting good things in

When your home could do with a slightly more thorough pick-me-up to lift the atmosphere, try this simple, practical remedy for an immediate change:

- Open the doors and windows while you tidy up
- Throw away rubbish, including any dead or dying flowers and plants
- Put away in a cupboard or drawer anything you dislike, find ugly or feel negative about
- Tidy up and put everything else away
- Light some incense to sweeten the place
- Ring a bell to brighten the atmosphere
- If possible, bring in some fresh flowers
- Close the windows and light a candle
- Put some music on
- Relax

When you want something different, try the following.

Flower power

This very simple ritual uses bells and flowers to clear away stale, negative energy and bring harmony and serenity in its place. Use often in the living room or any room that could benefit from gentle, frequent refreshing.

YOU WILL NEED:

A bell

A white candle

A bunch of fresh flowers – whatever appeals to you

Put the flowers in a vase. Light the candle and take a moment to focus on your intention – to bring peace and harmony into your home.

Move round the room ringing the bell. Imagine the sweet, clear sound dispelling any negativity. Then sit quietly with the candle and the flowers for a few moments and ask the spirit of peace to be present. Sense the clear, golden light from the candle flame gradually filling the whole room with radiance. Visualise soft sparks of love and harmony filling the place and being absorbed into the flowers until they radiate peace and tranquillity.

When you feel the ritual is complete, snuff the candle and put the flowers where they can be enjoyed.

Sense of Security

One of the things a soul home should provide is a sense of security. When you feel safe, your spirit can expand without worry.

Once you have made sure your house is physically secure, with good window locks, door lock, burglar alarm in working order, and such like, work on your sense of psychological security with some protection rituals.

Quick and simple psychic protectors include:

- GUARDIANS. It's surprising the number of houses you see with stone lions, eagles or dogs or even dragons on the gateposts, by the door or over the entrance. It's not confined to stately homes, either. Put a similar strong guardian presence in place to make your house feel protected

- AMULETS. Many old houses have something above the door, either inside or outside, to let good luck in and keep bad luck out. A horseshoe, rowan twig, carved cross, angel figure, star or similar good-luck charm could do the same for you

- DEFLECTORS. Hang glass balls and mirrors to deflect and turn aside bad luck, ill wishing and evil spirits

- SEALING RITUALS. Washing the doorstep or threshold of the home with salt water is traditionally said to prevent misfortune from entering. If you feel the outside world is intruding too much into your sanctuary, go round your house and paint the rune of protection, Elhaz Ý , with salt water on every entrance – doors, windows, TV, computer, phone, radio, etc

Candlelight shield

This is a slightly more elaborate sealing ritual.

YOU WILL NEED:

A white candle

A candle holder you can carry around safely

At dusk, light the candle and stand by the open front door of your house. Take a few moments to look into the flame and focus on what you are doing – bringing peace and protection to your home.

Imagine the candlelight gently expanding until a glowing sphere of radiance surrounds you. Focus your attention on the region of your heart and sense it relaxing and opening as you add the power of love to the candlelight. Shift your awareness downwards towards your diaphragm and feel your solar plexus opening and relaxing as you add courage and acceptance to the mix. Visualise the light expanding to fill every corner of the room while you say the words 'Peaceful and protected' to yourself.

Close the door and repeat in every room of your home.

Blessings

No soul home could be complete without blessings. Try these rituals to bring a sense of grace into your residence.

Blessing your home

YOU WILL NEED:

A large candle

Family photos or pictures of yourself if you have no family

Flowers

Incense

Glass of wine, or a non-alcoholic substitute such as spring water

Pen and paper

Gold ribbon

Sit somewhere in the centre or heart of your home. Arrange the candle, incense, flowers and photos on a low table to form a sort of mini-altar. Light the candle and the incense. Take a few moments to feel relaxed and comfortable and focus on what you intend to do – bring a sense of blessing into your home.

On the piece of paper, write down the address of your house followed by the names of the people who live there. Use the rest of the paper to write down all the things you would like to be present in your home and family, such as love, tolerance, laughter, abundance. Look at the photographs and think of all the good things you wish for the people there. (Don't forget to include yourself.)

Fold the paper and sprinkle a few drops of wine or water onto it, asking for the blessings of love, luck, light, goodness and wisdom. Tie the gold ribbon around it and put it on the altar amongst the flowers and photos. Toast with the wine or water saying, 'May all good things be in this place'. Imagine the candle flames beaming your wishes out into the universe.

Leave your mini-altar in place for the next few days. Re-light the candle every so often and recapture the feeling of wishing and blessing.

Blessing a new home

Get off to fresh start in a new home. It's a golden opportunity to break the connection with any past negative experiences and concentrate on building up a bright, positive future.

YOU WILL NEED:

Incense

A white candle

Glass of water

Small bowl of salt

A bell

A piece of bread

A potted plant

Start in the heart of your home, wherever you feel the true centre is – the living room, the kitchen, wherever. Light the candle and the incense. You could, if you like, light a candle in every room. Relax and take a few deep breaths. Feel the house resting quietly around you.

Take the water and walk through every room sprinkling a few drops in each with your fingers. Say to yourself, 'With this water I wash away all doubt and fear.' Next, take the bowl of salt and work your way through the house again, scattering a few grains in each room and saying, 'With this salt I purify all negativity.' Take the candle and visit each room in turn saying, 'With this light I bring love to drive out darkness.' Do the same with the incense saying, 'With this incense I bring sweetness and harmony.' Finally take the bell and ring it gently in each room saying, 'With this bell I summon all good things – joy, peace, love and laughter.' Eat half the bread and bury the rest in the plant pot saying, 'May abundance and prosperity grow here.'

Keep the plant in the heart of your home and tend it regularly.

This is Dedicated to…

When you want more of something in your life, dedicate a room to receiving it.

Create the right setting, add a little ritual to captivate your unconscious, and you begin to bring about the moods and feelings you desire in your home. Need a place to think? Dedicate a study area to clear-headedness and concentration. Want more romance? Ritually dedicate your bedroom to love.

When you dedicate a room to a particular thing, just going in there will automatically attune your mind to that purpose, and the more you do it, the stronger the connection becomes. Just repeat the ritual if you feel the connection fading.

A welcoming entrance

This is the first place you see when you get home. Make it a truly welcoming place.

- Mirrors increase the feeling of light and space
- Flowers provide a lift for the soul as you step through the door
- A cupboard or screen hides the off-putting muddle of coats most people have in their hall
- Soft, bright colours provide a contrast with the outside world
- Wind chimes will ring out a greeting when the door opens
- Well chosen pictures and objects establish the mood of your home and set the scene for what follows

Your entrance hall is the threshold of your home; it looks both inward and outward. In past time these 'in between' places were important. They marked the transition between one place and another, one state of mind and another.

The following ritual acknowledges this and makes your threshold the place where you let go of the outside world and enter into the spirit of home. Even if you don't have an entrance hall, make a 'welcome home' space just inside your front door and dedicate it to that important feeling of coming home.

Entrance hall

YOU WILL NEED:

*Glass of white wine or a non-alcoholic substitute
such as spring water*

White candle

White flowers – a bunch of flowers or a potted plant

*Statuette, picture or photograph to represent the
guardian spirit of your home*

The first task is to find something to represent the guardian spirit of your home. Choose something that gives you a warm feeling or that makes you smile. A ceramic ornament, wooden carving, a figurine, a gnome, fairy, god or goddess, dragon, earth mother, unicorn, African mask, totem animal – anything will do as long as it has character and 'speaks to you'. It can hang on the wall, sit on a shelf or dresser or dangle from the ceiling, but put it somewhere where you'll see it when you walk in through the door.

Put your chosen guardian in place. Arrange the flowers nearby and light the candle. Pour a glass of wine. You're now ready to dedicate your new guardian. Raise the glass and toast your guardian spirit with the words: 'To home. May love, peace and joy be in this place.' Take a sip from the glass then sprinkle a few drops from the glass onto your guardian spirit and a few more over your doorstep or door threshold.

Enjoy a little time in the candlelight, absorbing the quiet radiance of the light, the beauty of the flowers and the presence of your guardian. Focus on feeling really warm, welcomed and at home.

Every day, when you come through your front door, take a moment to greet your guardian and let them welcome you home. You could put a bowl or dish in front of your guardian where you leave your keys, loose change, etc., when you come in and where you will be able to find them again when you go out. As you drop your keys in the bowl, imagine dropping all the cares of the day along with them.

Bedrooms

Do you yearn for a sanctuary from the outside world, a place of enchantment where you can relax and feel good the moment you walk through the door?

Bedrooms are the place for love and dreams – for every pleasure from spiritual renewal to sensual delight. Dedicate your bedroom with ritual, but you might want to take some practical preparatory steps before you start.

- Clear out clutter. Find storage space for clothes, books, CDs, etc.
- Move out anything associated with work or worry. Computer, ironing board, tax files, study course notes and textbooks – they all have to find a new home.
- Make it comfortable. Cushions, covers, curtains, pictures and carpets all make a difference. Paint the walls a soft, warm shade of your favourite colour.
- Check the lighting. Soft light from bedside lamps is clearly more restful than a 100 watt bulb in the middle of the ceiling.

Try this rose-filled ritual to prepare your bedroom for love and romance. Before you start, collect together all the things you need for a truly sensual bedroom. What would you like – scented massage oils, candles, perfumes, silk cushions, fake-fur throw? Go on, treat yourself.

Rose magic

YOU WILL NEED:

Your collection of bedroom treats plus baskets, bowls or boxes to store and/or display them in

Incense

Three candles:

One to represent yourself – gold for males, silver for females

One to represent your partner – gold or silver as before

One pink candle for love. Choose the shade of pink to match your feelings, from pale pink for romance through to deepest crimson for passion (White symbolises spiritual love or a parent's love for a child)

A small sachet – made or bought – stuffed with dried rose petals

Three ribbons to match the colours of your candles

Light the incense and let the scent permeate the room while you just breathe it in and relax for a few moments. Light the candles. Sit on the bed with the rose-filled sachet and the ribbons. Visualise a warm pink light radiating from the candles, filling the room and everything in it with a soft glow. Let it enfold you as if you were in the heart of a rose.

Imagine pink rose petals raining softly down around you, filling your lap, spilling onto the bed, filling the room with their velvety sweetness. Breathe in their heady scent. Let it fill you with thoughts of romance and desire.

Ask the spirit of love (and passion, too, if you like) to be with you. Feel your own heart become warm with an answering love. Take the three ribbons and knot them together at one end. Plait the three lengths together as you visualise blending you, your partner and love into one indivisible thread. Tie the plaited ribbon around the sachet, tying the deep, rich energy of the rose into it.

Arrange your collection of sensuous treats around the room and put the sachet under your pillow to scent your dreams and desires.

Serenity magic

This next ritual will prepare your bedroom for serenity and rest, to help you renew your soul each night.

What would you have in a bedroom dedicated to rest and sleep? Treat yourself to whatever you desire – soft pillows, satin eye-mask, dream diary, silk sleepwear or cosy pyjamas, soothing CDs, scented candles – be totally self-indulgent.

YOU WILL NEED:

*Your bedtime treats plus baskets, bowls or boxes
to store and/or display them in*

Incense

Blue candle

*A small sachet - made or bought – stuffed with
dried camomile and lavender*

Some white feathers and a blue ribbon

Light the incense and let it waft through the room, dispersing
any lingering discord, ready for a softer energy. Light the blue
candle and sit quietly with the sachet, feathers and ribbon. As
the candle burns, visualise a soft, pearly light filling the room
and enveloping you in its quiet radiance. Imagine the light
falling like white feathers, soft as snowflakes drifting down,
landing lightly all round you. Angels' feathers filling the room
with gentleness. Imagine curling up in a nest of them,
completely comfortable, safe and warm.

Ask the spirit of peace and tranquillity to be with you and
sense an answering peace growing within your heart. Tie the
feathers into a bunch with the ribbon, and tie the ribbon
around the sachet, tenderly tying restfulness into it. Picture
feathers floating down on you, filling everything with peace.

Arrange your bedtime treats and put the sachet under your
pillow. Breathe in its scent to recapture that peacefulness.

Kitchens

Even today, the kitchen is often the heart of the home, but in
the past the hearth and its cooking pot were the vital centre

holding the family together. They were the hub round which the rest of life revolved. A well-tended fire and well-filled pot not only meant bodily warmth and nourishment, they also promised comfort and contentment, a respite from danger, nagging cold and hunger. The kitchen hearth was somewhere to relax – sated, satisfied and safe.

Dedicate your kitchen to these ancient principles of abundance and nurturing to keep your heart and spirit nourished as well as your body.

Kitchen warmth

What symbolises the truly abundant kitchen to you? It would probably be something different for everyone – an Aga, copper cooking pots, an overflowing fruit basket, a windowsill full of herbs.

Gather together the things that convey to you an unstinted sense of abundance and plenty along with some bright ceramic bowls and baskets to keep them in. I suggest you also find room for a bowl of brightly coloured fruits – oranges, red apples, kumquats and nectarines, for example, along with some living, growing herbs either in pots or growing in a window box.

YOU WILL NEED:

Your kitchen collection

Three orange candles

A toothpick, pin or something similar

Sit quietly and focus on your intention - to bring warmth and abundance into this kitchen to feed the soul as well as the body.

Take the three candles and inscribe one of the following runes on each:

- ◊ JERA – the rune for harvest
- ◊ ODAL – the rune for home
- ◊ INGUZ – the rune for fire

Light the candles. As they burn, imagine yourself back in that past era with firelight flickering on the walls. Outside there may be darkness, danger and the unknown, but here in this circle of light there is warmth and plenty – food for everyone and the promise of contentment.

Visualise the warm light growing, filling the room and driving back the darkness. Picture it pushing back cold and hunger and filling their place with warmth and satisfaction. Ask the spirit of the hearth fire to be with you, to feed and nurture you. Let the light into your heart and feel a growing sense of warmth and contentment. Let the light bless your kitchen and everything in it.

Arrange your new kitchen items. For the first meal you make after this ritual, re-light the orange candles during its preparation, using some of the herbs and fruit to flavour it.

Bathrooms

Bathrooms can be wonderfully healing places for body, mind and soul. Purifying and restoring, calming and nurturing, bathrooms provide a physical and spiritual sanctuary. Use this ritual to dedicate your bathroom to peace and make it an oasis for relaxation and recuperation.

Bathroom sanctuary

YOU WILL NEED:

Collect together all the things you would like in your bathroom oasis: candles for around the bath, scented bath oils, bath pillows, soaps, soft towels, lotions, potions and unguents – anything that symbolises comfort and luxury to you

Baskets, bowls or boxes to display these items in

Spray mister filled with rose water

Turquoise candle

Light the turquoise candle and focus on your intention – to dedicate this room to cleansing and to restoring body, mind and spirit. Mist the room with the water spray and enjoy the scent for a moment – gentle and refreshing as summer rain.

Visualise rays of soft, clear light radiating out from the candle flame, gently cleansing and purifying every corner of the room. Ask the spirit of healing to be with you. Breathe in the light and the scent and let your heart fill with serenity. Visualise the light expanding outwards, filling the room with tranquillity.

Arrange the soaps, oils, and any other items you have chosen, and perhaps finish by having a candle-lit bath.

Study areas

With more people than ever working and studying from home, it's important to have a place where you feel free to concentrate. Even if you can't spare a whole room, establish a definite place for study that allows you to dedicate that space to clear thinking, inspiration and creativity.

Treat yourself to all the things you really desire in your study area. What would you like? Beautiful notebooks, an elegant desk lamp, desk accessories, personalised mouse mat, CDs to help you concentrate? Don't forget to include symbols of what you have achieved, such as diplomas and awards, and pictures, photos and other symbols of what you want to accomplish in the future to help you towards your goals.

Study in peace

YOU WILL NEED:

Your collection of study aids plus something to store and/or display them in

Incense

A yellow candle

Rosemary essential oil

Light the incense and breathe in the scent for a few moments while thinking about your intention – to bring insight, clarity and inspiration into your study area.

Let the incense smoke dissolve any dullness or confusion, leaving the room clear and fresh. Waft the smoke towards your body. Fan it over your head and neck saying 'I cleanse my mind so I may think clearly.' Close your eyes and direct the smoke over your face saying 'I cleanse my eyes so I may see clearly and my tongue so I may speak truly.' Let the smoke envelop the rest of your body saying 'I cleanse my heart so I may be open to wisdom and my stomach so I have courage for the truth.'

Put a few drops of the rosemary oil onto the candle and light it. Visualise the light radiating out from the flame and penetrating deeply into your mind, illuminating and energising every brain cell, expanding your intellect and opening up new areas of thought and ideas.

Ask the spirit of wisdom to be with you. Breathe in the light and scent, and feel your mind and heart becoming calm, still and clear in response. Imagine illumination spreading outwards from your mind and filling the room.

Arrange your study aids ready for use. Keep the rosemary oil and sniff a little on a tissue when you need extra mental alertness.

Special Energy

When you feel a special affinity with something that has a particular symbolism for you – angels, say, or the moon or sun, rainbows or the natural elements – why not dedicate your home or a space within your home to these special energies?

- Angels are associated with a number of positive things – healing, joy and protection. They make a charming symbol for a happy home

- The moon is associated with feminine energies of intuition, magic and mystery. If you feel connected to lunar energies or would like more of their influence in your life, try a lunar ritual
- The sun symbolises light, joy, abundance, growth, happiness, etc. Who couldn't do with a little more of all those things in their life?
- Rainbows are believed by many to be the bridge between this world and the unconscious world of gods, goddesses and magical power. They bring hope, joy and delight into the home
- Elemental forces are the natural energies of the world – earth, water, fire and air. Bringing them into the home puts you in touch with the power of the natural world we live in

Entertaining angels

Whether you believe angels exist or not, there is no doubt living with angels, even just the idea of them, makes life much more fun. You might like to introduce joyful angel energy into the whole of your home, or just into one room – your bedroom, say, for protection and healing, or a child's room to guide and protect them.

YOU WILL NEED:

An angel figure – ceramic, glass, carved, crystal, whatever you like

Lavender or lilac candle

Four clear quartz crystals

Light the candle. Put a crystal in each corner of the room, or in each outer corner of the house if you prefer. Sit in the centre of the space and visualise a brilliant, pure white light beaming down into it. Imagine joy and laughter descending with the light.

Visualise your angel figure pulling in more and more brightness until the entire space is filled with love, light and laughter. Picture the four crystals at each corner holding it in place, anchoring it securely. (Angel energy is so light it needs holding down.)

Put your angel figure in a prominent place to watch over you. Light a lavender candle occasionally and spend some time visualising that brilliant white light descending. You may find your angel becomes somewhere to take your troubles and worries when they get too much for you.

If you like, you could begin collecting angels, as and when you see them, to decorate your space.

A place in the sun

Bring a little spiritual sunshine as well as the physical sort into your life with this ritual. It's especially good for lifting your spirits when the days are dark and gloomy and you feel down in the dumps. Try it during those last, dark days of winter when you find the first of the daffodils in your garden or in the shops.

Do it on a Sunday for extra symbolism.

A bunch of yellow flowers or a yellow pot plant

Yellow or gold candles – as many as you want, but at least three

Light the candles. Hold the flowers in your hands and gaze into them deeply, breathing in their scent and drawing their colour deeply into you.

Imagine you are becoming enveloped in a halo of golden light. As the golden colour begins to reach deeply into you, feel happiness and pleasure growing deep inside. Sense the colour and light filling you from head to toe, filling every inch of your body with bright golden yellow. Visualise it expanding beyond you, filling the room with golden sunshine. See your whole house overflowing with sunshine and happiness.

When you've finished, keep the flowers somewhere where you will see them often over the next few days. Collect sun symbols and yellow and gold flowers, candles, etc, to enhance the feeling of sun-power within your space.

Drawing down the moon

When you want a place that stimulates your feminine, intuitive side, or when you want to feel closer to bewitchment, mystery and magic, dedicate a space to the moon. Do it when the moon is full for extra symbolism, and if you can look at it while you work, even better.

Thirteen white stones (the moon has thirteen phases in a year)

Thirteen white candles

Arrange twelve of the stones in a circle big enough for you to stand in safely. Put the last stone in the centre. Place a candle behind each stone and light them all – go clockwise round the circle and light the centre one last.

Stand or sit (depending on how much room you have) in the middle of the circle. Imagine drawing the power and light of the moon down into the circle. Visualise a soft, silvery light descending, and draw it deeply into yourself.

Imagine you are encircled by a sphere of silver light and feel wisdom, beauty and grace growing deep inside. Draw the delicate light deeper inside you and sense it filling every fibre of your body, increasing your sensitivity and perception. Visualise it expanding beyond you to fill the room with silver. See your whole house overflowing with this magical light.

Collect moon symbols and arrange them along with white, silvery blue and lilac candles, flowers, and such like, to enhance the lunar feeling of the room.

The rainbow room

Rainbows bring a fiery energy. They are associated with hope and renewal and will brighten the drabbest, dullest atmosphere.

YOU WILL NEED:

Seven candles – one for each colour of the rainbow:

Red

Orange

Yellow

Green

Light blue

Dark blue

Violet

Seven flowers – one for each colour of the rainbow also

Light the red candle and hold the red flower in your hand. Gaze deeply into it, breathing in any scent it has and drawing the colour deeply into you.

Become enveloped in a halo of jewel-red light and sense it filling every cell in your body. Visualise it expanding, filling the room and then your whole house. Move on to the orange candle and flower and repeat, then go on the yellow, and then all the other colours in turn. Bathe yourself and your home in successive waves of glorious colour.

Afterwards, hang crystals (glass prisms) in every window that catches the sun and watch the rainbows dance when the sun shines.

Attracting the elements

Bring the power of the elements – earth, water, fire and air – into your home:

- WATER symbolises cleansing and healing. It is associated with the emotions and its power promotes empathy and strong emotional health

- EARTH is connected with nurturing, strength and 'at-homeness'. Its power promotes stability and safety and gives your home strong roots

- AIR is symbolic of inspiration. It is invigorating and refreshing and promotes clear communication. A home with the power of air in it will never feel stale or dull

- FIRE represents energy, passion and spirit. It brings light and life into the home and also protects it

  YOU WILL NEED:

  A red candle for fire

  A bowl of water for water

  Incense for air

  A potted herb or flower for earth

Light the candle, and as you sit and look at it imagine you feel the flame attracting the power of fire into the room. Feel its warmth and energy as you say to yourself, 'May the transforming, warming energy of fire light up my home.'

Hold the bowl of water in your hands and sense it drawing in the spirit of water as you remember the healing powers of the sea, of summer rain, of a hot bath. Feel yourself relax as you say, 'May the healing, flowing power of water soothe my home.' Sprinkle a few drops of water around the room.

Light the incense. Let the smoke drift through the room as you visualise the spirit of air flowing in and blowing away all the spiritual cobwebs. Say, 'May the breath of life be in my home.'

Finally, take the flowers or plant in your hands and imagine you feel it drawing the power of the earth into your space. Sense the power of green things growing, and the solidity of firm bedrock. Say, 'May the strength and abundance of earth support my home.'

Remind yourself of the elements when you decorate your home. Bring in natural things rather than man-made objects and choose things to symbolise the four powers.

- WATER – bowls of water with floating candles or flowers; pictures of the sea and sea creatures; interior waterfalls and pools; aquariums; shells; water-polished stones and driftwood. Use a plant mister to spray scented water around the room

- EARTH – potted herbs and flowers; indoor gardens; stone and earthenware vessels; bowls of fruit and nuts; terracotta figures and pots; natural crystals; wooden objects; pictures of flowers, gardens and landscapes

- AIR – incense; wind chimes; woodwind and flute music; bird and butterfly ornaments; feathers; pictures featuring wide expanses of sky. Open the windows at least once every day

- FIRE – candles. Open up your fireplace and have a real hearth

Ordinary Magic

With imagination and a touch of ritual, the most ordinary things around the house become tools for spiritual development and inspiration for the soul.

Telephone

Near the phone is a good place to keep photos of friends and family. You can look at them as you speak to them.

If you know a difficult phone call is coming up, put something inspiring – a picture or object that either energises you or keeps you calm – by the phone to lift your spirits while you talk.

If you frequently speak to someone you have difficulties with on the phone, see if you can find a photo of them looking happy and relaxed and keep it handy. Seeing them looking positive while you are talking to them might ease the problem.

If you find talking on the phone difficult in general, put a photo of yourself smiling and looking confident where you can see it as you speak.

Mail

Everyone likes getting letters. Write wishes, affirmations and blessings and post them to yourself so you get a little magic in the morning mail.

When you're going through a difficult patch, send yourself

cards with cheering messages written in them. There's something about getting them through the post that makes them especially effective.

Key

Every home seems to have at least one mysterious key that doesn't fit any of the locks in the house. Use this key as a personal talisman. Clean it and either attach it to a suitably symbolic key ring or thread it on a ribbon. Keep it to remind you to be open – open-hearted, open-minded and open-handed.

Iron

Ironing can be very therapeutic. Visualise smoothing out all the problems on your path in life as you smooth out the creases. If you have an interview or important meeting, press your clothes with special care and visualise the meeting running just as smoothly.

Feather duster

If a room feels dull, dismal and lacking in energy, dust round energetically with a feather duster to tickle it up and lighten the atmosphere. It's almost impossible to do this without finding yourself smiling by the end of it.

Vacuum cleaner

Visualise sucking up all the negativity in your home –

arguments, upsets, disagreements and quarrels – along with the dust as you vacuum.

Magnet

Magnets attract. Use fridge magnets with appropriate symbols – they come in all shapes, sizes and designs – to draw the things you want into your life.

See Chapter 5 for more ideas about what you can achieve with some basic kitchen equipment and a good imagination.

Chapter Four

Magical Places

Celebrate your soul

If you want an enchanted life, one way to bring this about is to build an altar. An altar is one of the best and simplest tools for practising enchanted living I know of, hence their popularity in nearly every culture throughout history.

Altars provide a focal point. They're a visible expression of thoughts and feelings. They give form to the formless whether that's divine spirit or your own needs and desires. Just making one for yourself is an uplifting experience. There's something deep inside the human soul that wants to make places of beauty and celebration – visible hymns to life and spirit.

Even a tiny corner-of-a-shelf altar can have a profound effect on you. It can:

- Remind you of the good things in your life
- Remind you who you are and what you want to be
- Express your wishes and desires

- Strengthen your resolution and motivation
- Revive your flagging will-power

Divine Shrines and Altared States

Wouldn't it be wonderful to have a space, however small, dedicated solely to what was most important to you? Wouldn't you like to have a place where you could find tranquillity, inspiration, balm for your soul and spiritual connection whenever you needed it?

An altar is just such a place. When you build an altar (or two; or three) you are making a place where you focus on, and energise, aspects of yourself and your life – from the highest, most spiritual and divine to the most basic and commonplace.

When you introduce an altar into your life, you are making somewhere where you pause to appreciate, celebrate and remember. But what altars chiefly do is help you focus on something specific. When you build an altar to something, it's a signal to your unconscious mind you're taking it very seriously indeed. Consider the following examples.

DO YOU HAVE A GOAL IN LIFE?

Do you want to write a novel? Start a business? Have a career? Travel to exotic lands? Live the life you've always dreamed of? Build an altar to it. Spend time with it, light candles, light incense, bring flowers – your unconscious mind will soon start to take your objectives seriously.

DO YOU WANT TO CHANGE SOMETHING?

Whether it's something about yourself or about your circumstances you want to transform, an altar covered with symbols of that change will kick-start your energy, concentrate your mind and strengthen your resolve to help you bring it about.

DO YOU WANT TO VALUE SOMETHING MORE HIGHLY?

Do you want to give more time, more value to your family, your friends, your spiritual life, the natural world, the community around you? Build an altar. Your unconscious will ensure it soon takes a more prominent role in your life.

DO YOU WANT TO VALUE SOMETHING ABOUT YOURSELF MORE?

Your masculinity or femininity? Your creativity? Your role as a parent? Your courage, friendliness, intuition or openness? Your ethnic origin? Build an altar, put beautiful things on it that represent you and see how you grow in your own estimation.

DO YOU WANT TO CELEBRATE SOMETHING?

Is there something in your life that makes you feel joyful that you simply want to spend time thinking about and enjoying? Build an altar and spend happy times there. Recharge your spiritual batteries.

DO YOU WANT MORE OF SOMETHING?

What would you like more of in your life? Love; health; blessings; courage; abundance; peace; solace; energy? Build an altar – concentrate on your needs and take them seriously. Don't let your desires languish, formless and nebulous, give them a visible appearance you can focus on.

Nothing is so big or so small you can't build an altar to it if you want to. On the contrary, altars seem to have the effect of making the little things more significant while bringing the big things within reach. Nothing is too basic or mundane, either – the best altars are those which simply fit into your everyday life, bringing a moment of joy or focus that becomes part of your daily schedule. I have a bee altar in the room where I work, decorated with representations of bees; hives and honeycombs, a jar of honey, beeswax candles and so on. To me, it represents contented and industrious workers. When I feel stressed or bored or overwhelmed with work, a few minutes at the altar (and a spoonful of honey) soon reminds me of the sweet rewards of industry and restores my flagging motivation.

You don't have to fill your house with altars, though you might find them so useful and inspiring that you'll want to. You'll probably find, as you read this chapter, one or two types of altar will take root in your imagination or answer some current need – try those first. As your needs change, dismantle your altar and build another. Or maybe you'll find some niche or corner that's just crying out for a magic focal point. Or perhaps something new will come into your life you want to celebrate.

If you're still unsure about the power of altars, try this simple experiment. Find a small space where you can safely set up:

- A white candle
- Something with the word 'Peace' written on it with a silver pen – a card, smooth pebble, or whatever takes your fancy
- A small glass where you put a flower

Every day, take a few minutes to visit this tiny altar:

- Light the candle
- Put a fresh flower in the glass
- Read the word 'Peace', and repeat it to yourself a few times

See how you feel after doing this every day for a week.

Making an Altar

Build your altar anywhere. (Build them everywhere!) You don't have to set aside a special room. If you're like most people, you probably have an 'unofficial' altar already. You could even have several. A collection of family photographs on a mantelpiece; postcards and mementoes of happy times pinned to a bulletin board; souvenirs of a holiday displayed on a shelf – all of them somewhere where you pause in the course of a busy day to appreciate, celebrate and remember. These are the beginnings of a rudimentary altar.

An altar doesn't have to be large or elaborate; a table, a stool, the top of a chest, a shelf, even an upturned box will do at a push. It can be as unobtrusive as you like or, if you prefer, really go to town and make a feature of it.

Table-top altars

Table-top altars are the easiest to create. Pick a table – high, low, round, square, coffee, whatever – or a stool. Throw a piece of fabric or a scarf across it and arrange the rest of your things on top. Keep it for as long as you want. It can be permanent, semi-permanent, or just until you need to use the table.

Portable altars

An altar in a box you can set up as and when you need it, wherever you are, has a certain appeal, especially if you travel a lot.

Find a nice box and pack it with a scarf or handkerchief (to use as an altar cloth), some tiny candles, a few sticks of incense and an incense-burner, along with essential symbolic items. You can unpack and set up your temporary shrine in a hotel room or wherever, and then even the most impersonal place has a soothing, calming centre.

Shelf-top shrines

Clear a shelf and dedicate it for use as an altar. It can be a display shelf or, if you value privacy, it could be a shelf in a cupboard. Set up your shrine as you want it, then just open the door and it's there ready, whenever you like. Be extra careful with candles in enclosed spaces, though.

Window ledges offer similar possibilities.

Alcoves

Moving on to slightly more permanent arrangements, niches and alcoves make attractive settings for altars. You could put a table or chest there, or fix up a shelf. Paint the alcove a suitable colour for your intended purpose and decorate it however you like. An alcove, of course, gives you the opportunity to hang things on the wall and from the ceiling as well as arrange things on top of the altar.

Permanent altars

You might find you want to dedicate a permanent space to keep solely as an altar – a whole room, a screened corner or niche, or even a garden shed or summerhouse. (Yes, they do exist. How about a greenhouse shrine to growth, fertility and the essence of nature?)

Permanent altars give you a lot of scope for decoration and embellishment to get the atmosphere exactly right. Take into account the needs and activities of others in your home and how private or public you want to be. You might want to consider the traditional places where household shrines are found in other cultures – the kitchen, hearth and threshold. Do you want it to be part of your everyday life, or do you want to set it apart for special times and visits?

What goes on an altar?

Your altar is your power place. It's the place you go to calm your mind, delight your soul, strengthen your resolve and renew your courage, amongst other things. It's important your altar is personal to you and that the things that go on it have a personal and precious meaning for you.

Personal items

The most important objects on your altar will be the personal things that embody the purpose of your altar – the objects, figures, ornaments, pictures, words, and photographs that capture your imagination and have a special meaning for you. Be adventurous and don't be afraid to experiment, you can always change things.

SYMBOLS

What is your altar for? If, for example, your altar celebrates your family, you would probably choose photos of your relatives and loved ones, along with items that remind you of them, such as personal items and treasured mementoes. You could also include symbols of love and protection such as angels, hearts, stars and so on. If your altar is dedicated to a goal in life, choose symbols of that goal along with words and affirmations to inspire you.

Whatever you choose, you can always change them or add new items as your thoughts, feelings and ideas change. Let your altar grow and evolve continuously over time.

MEMENTOES

Personal items and mementoes contribute greatly. An altar dedicated to strengthening your confidence, for example, might include reminders of events or occasions when you felt confident. Souvenirs you've collected through the years, and their associated memories, give a great deal of meaning to an altar. A meaningful gift carries all the love that accompanied it when it was given. Gifts and keepsakes from friends and relatives also carry wonderful memories.

AFFIRMATIONS

Putting words on your altar helps bring home the message to your unconscious, whether the words are prayers and blessings, poems, affirmations, or just single words of inspiration.

PICTURES

Pictures and photos bring a strong visual image to your altar, something for you, literally, to focus on.

Photographs from the family album, for instance, could help

you cultivate a constructive relationship with your past if that's what you need. You can also use photos, cards and illustrations to bring the qualities the pictures represent to your altar. A picture that embodies a quality you admire or desire – tranquillity, gentleness, joy, friendship, etc – could help you find that quality in yourself. A picture of someone or something you find inspiring could encourage you during tough times and help you get through them.

Symbolic items

In addition to personal items, there are other items that are useful for altar building. Particular examples for specific altars are gone into in detail later in this chapter, but, briefly, you might consider including the following.

NATURAL OBJECTS

Stones, shells, pieces of driftwood, acorns, horse chestnuts, feathers and pinecones all seem to find their way into our pockets at some time or another. We just seem to have an urge to collect natural things. Use them on your altar, if you wish, to remind you:

- Of the walk you took; where you were and who you were with, when you picked them up
- Of the freedom of being in the open air
- Of the generosity and abundance of nature
- Of the peaceful beach, shady wood, etc where you

found them
- Of the flight of birds, the strength of trees, the age of rocks, etc

THE FOUR ELEMENTS

The four elements remind us of our origins and the four fundamental powers of the universe – earth, water, fire and air. For this reason, many altars, whatever their purpose, include representations of the elements.

Fire – candles, mirrors, flame colours
Water – bowl of spring water, shells
Earth – stones, bowl of earth or sand, salt, wood, herbs, flowers
Air – feathers, birds, butterflies, incense, a flute

Represent each element separately, or think up beautiful ways to combine them. Fill a clear glass bowl with water, for example, and float flowers and candles on it to unite earth, water and fire.

SPIRITUAL REPRESENTATIVES

Many altars include figures representing deities or spiritual messengers such as angels. These give comfort and hope as well as representing attributes we want to include in our lives. My bedroom altar, for example, includes a figure of the Chinese Goddess Kwan Yin to remind me to be kind.

You could also include the sun and the moon as natural deities. The sun representing light, joy, reason, clarity, health, courage and strength; while the moon represents wisdom, intuition, change, sensitivity and perception.

TOTEM ANIMALS

Like spiritual representatives, animal totems embody qualities we desire. Be clear about what the animal symbolises to you, though. To some people cats symbolise independence, grace and mystery; to others they represent selfishness and deviousness. Some people feel the dog is a symbol of loyalty and courage, while others see it as a symbol of conformity and subservience. In general, though, some animals seem to crop up with a clear symbolic significance again and again.

LION – courage, proper pride, power
BEAR – strength, protection (especially of children)
WOLF – wisdom, leadership
DEER – grace, agility, speed (physical, mental, or emotional)
COW – domestic harmony, comfort
PIG – honesty, cleverness, humility
HORSE – freedom, energy
GOAT – confidence, surefootedness
HARE – intuition, inspiration
DOLPHIN – playfulness, wisdom
FROG – at home in two worlds, adaptability

SNAKE – creativity, energy, renewal
DOVE – peace, spirituality
CROW – intelligence, moving on
SWAN – grace (physical and spiritual)
EAGLE – vision, power, courage
OWL – wisdom, perception
BUTTERFLY – transformation, light-heartedness
SPIDER – creativity and persistence

MYTHICAL CREATURES

Mythical creatures are also powerful symbols and work strongly on the unconscious through the power of legend.

DRAGON – energy for transformation, life force
UNICORN – purity, strength through gentleness
PHOENIX – rebirth
FAIRY – communion with nature, inner child
WINGED HORSE – spiritual freedom, inspiration, spiritual communication

Decorative items

Once the symbolic things are in place, go to town on decorating your altar. Make it feel special right from the start.

ALTAR CLOTH

A beautiful cloth or mat is a great way of saying this is a special place. Your choice of colour, texture and decoration for your altar cloth will make a big difference to the overall mood of your altar. A plain white linen cloth, for example, gives a very different message to your unconscious than a gold embroidered, jewel-encrusted brocade.

CANDLES

To include candles on an altar almost goes without saying. Just lighting a candle creates a different mood. Select your candles to match your purpose. There are an almost infinite variety to choose from: tall, slender tapers for high ideals; star-shaped ones; scented ones; special *feng shui* candles; votive candles ... Think about colour and its symbolism too.

WHITE or natural beeswax – purity, spirituality

RED – enthusiasm, passion, energy, celebration

PINK – love, romance, gentleness, childhood

YELLOW – joy, luck, sunshine, friendship, communication

GREEN – healing, harmony, nature, fertility and abundance

BLUE – peace, meditation

VIOLET or PURPLE – spirituality, deep introspection, intuition

FLOWERS

Fresh flowers bring life to your altar. A potted plant, small posy or even a single flower will bring grace and colour. Again, you can, if you wish, choose them to suit your purpose.

Roses – love, romance
Lilies – purity, peace
Orchids – spiritual grace
Daisies – innocence
Marigolds – joy, sunshine, courage
Lotus – if you can get them, symbolise spiritual
enlightenment, rising above the darkness into light
Spring flowers – hope, new beginnings, faith
Summer flowers – abundance
Autumn flowers – introspection, continuation

INCENSE

Light a stick of incense and watch the smoke drift and curl. It's practically an act of meditation in itself, and scent goes straight to the emotion-and-memory part of the brain. Have something scented on your altar. Incense sticks are the easiest, but you could use incense cones or loose blends you burn on a charcoal block, or you could use an aromatherapy oil burner and scent your space with pure essential oils.

Using your altar

Now you've got it, what do you do with it? If your altar is going to be of any use to you, you have to use it and use it regularly. The rituals carried out at altars focus on:

- Purification
- Dedication
- Invocation

Purification

Make the place you have chosen for your altar feel special, by doing one or more of the following.

- Ring bells
- Burn incense and waft the smoke over it
- Sprinkle spring water with a sprig of lavender
- Scatter salt
- Spray with scented water
- Light candles
- Light an aromatherapy oil burner

Dedication

When you build an altar you are giving your dreams and desires a physical expression. When you concentrate on a particular goal in this way, you refine and intensify your will-power so it becomes a laser beam – cutting through the barriers that stopped you achieving your dreams in the past.

Before you start doing rituals at your altar, remind yourself what it's for. Dedicate it to that specific purpose.

Dedication ritual

YOU WILL NEED:

Your altar

Pen and paper (several sheets, or use cards)

Ribbon to match the colours on your altar

Candles, incense, flowers and anything else that feels celebratory to decorate with

Decorate the shrine with flowers and whatever else you have. Light the candles and incense. Take a few moments to sit at your altar and remember your specific purpose for making it. Ask yourself things like:

- What's my reason for building this altar?

- What results do I hope for?

- How will I know when I've achieved them?

Write down your answers to these questions as a 'statement of intent'. Fold or roll your statement, tie it with the ribbon and keep on the altar.

Check that what's on your altar contributes to your goal. If, for example, your shrine is dedicated to increasing your feelings of love and connection to your family, but you've included a picture of someone you dislike or feel uneasy with, they will stand in the way of that goal. Move the photo to a different place and work on establishing a better relationship with them separately.

Write out cards with words, wishes, prayers, affirmations, quotes and poems describing your dreams and aspirations and place them on the altar.

Take a couple of slow, deep breaths and focus on your heart. Visualise a light there that expands to encompass both you and your altar in a pure, clear radiance.

State your purpose for your altar, saying something like, 'May this altar be a place of peace to bring tranquillity into my life.' Or 'Let this altar remind me of my courage and determination and bring great strength into my life.' Or 'May this altar honour my family and remind me of the love and joy they bring into my life.' Or 'Let this altar honour my goal of bringing travel and adventure into my life.'

Acknowledge any spiritual representatives you have included, and give thanks for what you already have.

Invocation

Now your altar is ready for use. So what do you do? How do you use it? Altars work best when they're incorporated into the everyday pattern of your life. You can:

- Light a candle there for a few minutes morning and/or evening
- Light incense and enjoy the scent
- Leave a flower there when you pass
- Post wishes, prayers and affirmations there
- Put objects and pictures there as and when you come across them
- Repeat an affirmation as you pass
- Kneel and say a few words of blessing or thanks

It also helps if you regularly make time to enjoy a longer ritual at your shrine.

Invocation ritual

YOU WILL NEED:

Flowers, candles, incense, etc

Something to use as an offering – more flowers, fruit, natural object, cakes, wine, etc

You may also want a pen and paper

Purify your altar (see *Purification*, above). Light the candles and incense or an essential oil burner. Visualise that clear, radiant light expanding from your heart to surround both you and your altar and re-dedicate the shrine to its purpose (see above).

Put your offerings on the altar with a prayer of thanks and blessing. Picture your heart opening to absorb the atmosphere of your altar – the symbols you have put there, any spiritual representative you have included, such as totem animals and mythical creatures.

If time allows, go on to do one or more of the following (as described below): pray, repeat an affirmation, repeat a mantra, visualise, meditate. Whatever you choose to do, when you get towards the end of your session at your altar, decide on one action you'll take as a result of your prayers, meditation or visualisation and write it down. Read it to yourself and allow the light from your heart to encompass it. However small they are, actions as well as intentions are important to achieving your desires.

PRAYER

Prayer is a way of focusing. As with any heartfelt plea, the actual words you use are far less important than your sincerity. Speak out loud, or quietly within your heart, the important thing is you say what you truly feel.

You can pray for guidance, help, thanks, understanding or solace, and you can invoke a variety of spiritual helpers, depending on your beliefs and traditions.

- DEITIES – Deities and spiritual representatives, whether ancient or modern, often embody needs that can't be expressed by more everyday means. Call on them when you feel you need the help of a higher power
- YOUR HIGHER SELF – You can also call upon your higher self for guidance and strength. Your higher self is the best part of you – wise, generous and loving. Call on it when you want to move beyond doubt and suspicion, fear and worry, judgement and self-pity, negativity and limiting beliefs. Tap into it, too, when you want to invoke your joyful, loving and creative self
- SPIRITUAL GUIDES – Call directly to the spirit of love, the spirit of peace, the spirit of healing, etc – whatever quality you need to invoke. You can also call on people, saints, heroes and heroines who you feel embody those qualities. Call on them especially when you are struggling with specific issues
- ANCESTRAL SPIRITS – Many cultures throughout history have honoured their ancestors with shrines and altars and found strength and solace there. Like wise

grandparents, ancestral spirits are always ready to help, especially when you are dealing with family concerns

- TOTEM ANIMAL – Even if you haven't included a totem or mythical animal on your altar, you can still call upon their power to assist you. For example, when you need to be clear-sighted, call to the spirit of the hawk; when you know you'll need to be clever or cunning, call on the spirit of the fox
- ANGELS – Call on the angels for grace and blessing. As with spiritual guides, call on specific angels to endow you with specific qualities – the angel of wisdom, say, or the angel of adventure or the angel of joy. Invoke your personal guardian angel for spiritual grace and guidance

REPEAT AN AFFIRMATION

As well as writing affirmations and leaving them on your altar, use your time there to drive the message home to yourself. Repeat one over and over again in a kind of chant, either out loud or silently. Keep it positive, keep it short and aim to say it sincerely with your heart rather than just letting it float over the surface of your mind. Examples might include:

- I feel happy, I feel healthy, I feel terrific. Good things are coming to me right now.
- The perfect job is coming into my life right now.
- I am loved and I am loving. My heart is open.
- I am calm, happy and relaxed.

If angry, sad, bitter or cynical thoughts bubble up as a result, acknowledge them but keep repeating your affirmation until these negative thoughts settle and you let them go.

REPEAT A MANTRA

Even shorter than an affirmation, a mantra is a single word repeated over and over again. Either choose a word you already have on your altar or one that suits your needs. 'Calm', 'Peace' or 'Love', for example.

Breathe in slowly through your nose and out through your mouth. As you breathe out, let your word flow out with it – spoken, whispered or totally silent, whatever you prefer.

VISUALISE

Close your eyes and imagine achieving what you desire. See yourself enjoying your goal, hear the things you'll hear when you get there, feel the positive thoughts and emotions you'll experience. If, for example, your altar is dedicated to your goal of becoming a singer, focus your attention on the things that symbolise this for you, then close your eyes and visualise yourself doing exactly those things.

MEDITATE

No words, no prayers, no affirmations, just open your heart and your mind and listen to the voice within yourself. Listen in silence.

Everyday altars

Everyday altars are little shrines around the house and garden where you can stop off for some spiritual sustenance as you go about your daily round. They give enchantment to any life.

Heart of your home

Give your house a spiritual focal point – somewhere to express your desires, hopes and dreams for your home and your life there. Make it in the centre of your house. Either, literally, in the physical centre, or in the psychological centre – the place where people spend most time or naturally gravitate to. You could also build it in the bedroom – home of feelings and intuition.

Choose an altar cloth that reflects your ideal home whether that's rich, earthy, simple, quirky, elegant or magnificent. On it, put all the things that symbolise a truly happy home to you. Include the following.

- Affirmations, poems, words, pictures, photos and objects that represent everything you want to have in your home:
  - Material things
  - Events and occasions
  - Occupations and pastimes
  - The mood and tone
  - People
  - Feelings
  - Hopes and dreams

- Something to ground your altar and give it a feeling of weight and solidity – a natural object, earthenware pot, stone or smooth pebble.
- Lots of candles to echo the spirit of the hearth
- Someone or something to protect your home – an angel, deity or totem animal
- Something to characterise the spiritual element – a spiritual representative, deity, patron saint, angel, sun, moon, written blessing or prayer

Keep your home altar dynamic and alive. Bring fresh flowers and offerings frequently, light candles and burn incense. Leave wishes, prayers and affirmations. Chant a mantra there occasionally.

Room altars

Use altars in other rooms in your home to remind you of what you want and how you want to feel. Light a candle or two and repeat an affirmation to put you in the right frame of mind.

BEDROOM

Bedroom altars are often dedicated to either tranquillity, love or passion.

TRANQUILLITY

Choose soft, peaceful colours, such as blues and violets, for your altar cloth, candles, etc. Include pictures and illustrations of soothing scenes that calm and relax you. Write words and affirmations about sleep and peace such as 'Calm', 'Dream', 'Serene', etc. Keep a dream diary there. Have an angel or other guardian spirit to watch over you.

Spend a little time there before sleep to wind down and get you in the right mood. Repeat the affirmation, 'I summon the spirit of tranquillity here now'. (Remember to snuff candles and incense before you drift off.)

Love

Choose warm pinks for your cloth and candles. Include hearts of all sorts and sizes, roses and other flowers, cupids and valentine cards. Add pictures and illustrations that suggest love to you, photos of you and your partner as a couple (if appropriate) and mementoes of romantic occasions. Don't forget the gods and goddesses of love, and include lots of affirmations, such as 'I am loved and loving', 'Love', 'My heart is open'.

Spend time there with candles and flowers. Bring souvenirs and keepsakes to remind you of a loving relationship and of renewing that sense of love within yourself. Try repeating the affirmation, 'I summon the spirit of love here now', along with your own personal affirmations and mantras.

Passion

Hot pinks, purples, scarlet and crimson are the colours of passion. Choose sensuous textures and shapes for everything on your altar, lush flowers and intoxicating incense. It's also a good place to keep love letters, massage oils, and such like.

Light candles, breathe in incense, repeat a suitable affirmation or mantra to put you in the mood. 'I summon the spirit of passion here now ', works well.

KITCHEN

Make a kitchen altar dedicated to wellbeing and plenty. Use it to create a feeling of abundance in your life. Choose colours, shapes and textures that suit your kitchen, whether that's farmhouse rustic or sleek and streamlined. Load it up with symbols and affirmations of abundance – bowls of ripe fruit, lush plants and herbs, pictures that represent plenty to you and words such as 'Abundance', 'Wealth', 'Opulence', 'Sumptuous', 'Lavish', 'Lush', 'Fulsome' or 'Generous'. Keep rich spices and luxury treats there.

Add an Earth Mother figure, laughing Buddha, or similar representative of the spiritual face of abundance.

Bring luxurious offerings of wine and food to lay on your altar before you enjoy them. Light lots of candles, repeat an affirmation or mantra. Enjoy what you have.

BATHROOM

Healing, wholeness and renewal makes a good dedication for a bathroom altar. Choose relaxing, calming colours for your altar cloth, and include pure white candles. Include at least one flourishing potted plant, and vibrant pictures and illustrations. Write affirmations with words like 'Healing', 'Renewal' and 'Restored' in them. Keep your most luxurious soaps, salts and bath oils there, and have an angel or other healing spirit to watch over you.

The dolphin is a good totem animal to have on such an altar. So is the snake. Visualise shedding your old skin and emerging new, supple and gleaming. Butterflies are good, too. Again, visualise cracking open that dull, restrictive cocoon and letting your glorious wings spread out.

LIVING ROOM

The living room makes good place for a family altar. Use it to celebrate the people (and pets) in your life and create feelings of connection to them. Choose the colours, shapes and textures that fit naturally into your decor. As well as putting family photographs there, you could also include mementoes and keepsakes, along with pictures, words and objects that represent your wishes and hopes for your family and friends. It's a good place to keep things like birthday reminders and personal address books, too. Include a photo of yourself looking happy and add a guardian spirit to watch over all of you.

When someone is particularly in your thoughts for any reason, use your 'altar time' to focus on them, with maybe a prayer or meditation.

Bring flowers to put on your altar, and it's particularly nice to light candles on people's birthdays and special occasions.

GARDEN ALTARS

Altars don't only have to be indoors, garden shrines have their own unique charm. Use a flat stone, low wall or rockery, or garden table as a base, plant flowers and herbs around it and decorate it with weatherproof ornaments, wind chimes and natural objects. Pictures are difficult, but you can paint or carve words and affirmations on wood or stones. Water works well at a garden shrine. Pools, ponds and other water features form their own kind of focal point that make them a natural place for contemplation and also give you somewhere to float flowers and candles.

Include somewhere to sit, and bring candles and incense with you.

Altars for change

An altar can help you achieve your goals. It physically represents and externalises your hopes, dreams and desires, instead of leaving them to swim around in your mind, formless and vague. An altar helps you focus on what you want and what you need to do to achieve it.

Goals

Build altars dedicated to specific goals and aspirations. Collect together all the objects and pictures you can find that represent your particular goal. Think about:

- The physical things associated with that goal
- The thoughts and feelings you have about it

You might also want to consider including:

- Role models, heroes and heroines who have achieved what you aspire to
- Affirmations that will help you achieve results
- Spirit helpers and allies such as angels, patron saints, gods and goddesses, who will give you psychological and spiritual support
- Totem animals that possess the strengths and characteristics you will need

For example, an altar dedicated to the goal of writing a novel might include:

- Books, paper and writing materials
- The picture or book of a favourite novelist
- Your written promise to write a thousand words a day
- Pictures showing people reading, looking happy and absorbed
- A photo of you looking happy
- A statue of Athena, Goddess of Wisdom
- The figure of Ganesha, God of Creativity

- Totem spider web to symbolise the spinning of enchantment
- Appropriate affirmations

Add flowers, candles, incense and anything else you like. Use this altar as you would any other. Purify and re-dedicate it regularly, spend a little time there every day to strengthen your resolve and prime your unconscious to be on the lookout for opportunities for you. Bring offerings and leave prayers, wishes and affirmations as you like.

Spend time on longer rituals when you are able. Use your time at your altar to meditate, pray and visualise strongly what it will be like when you have achieved your goal. Aim to come up with at least one small step you can take towards your goal each time you perform an altar ritual.

Self-esteem

Make an altar that values and celebrates you or some aspect of your personality or character. Few things build up your confidence and self-esteem better. Include:

- All your favourite colours on the altar
- Celebratory-looking gold and/or silver candles
- Lots of affirmations – 'I am a good person', 'I am loveable and loving', 'I freely celebrate my creativity', 'My heart is open to myself', and so on
- A photo of you looking happy

- Lots of flowers
- Symbols of your hobbies and passions
- Representations of things you have achieved – certificates, awards, prizes
- Photos of friends
- Photos of your family
- A list of your strengths
- A list of your blessings
- Deity or spiritual representative who you respect
- A totem animal representing the strengths you are proud of

Spend at least a short time every day celebrating and affirming yourself. Your birthday is an excellent occasion to set up and dedicate such an altar.

Personal change

When you want to change something about yourself or your circumstances, spend a little time every day at an altar dedicated to just that. An altar will give your desires physical expression and focus your mind – conscious and unconscious – on the specific change you want to make.

When you're planning your altar, consider:

- What it is you want to change
- How you will be different when you've accomplished that change

Gather together things that represent the change you want to make:

- The physical things associated with that change
- Things that symbolise the change you want
- The thoughts and feelings you have about the change

Other things it would be useful to have include:

- Affirmations that will help you achieve the result you want
- Role models, heroes and heroines who represent the change you seek
- Spirit helpers and allies, such as angels, patron saints, gods and goddesses, who will give you psychological and spiritual support
- Totem animals that possess the strengths and characteristics you will need

For example, an altar dedicated to changing the way you eat – so your diet is healthier – might include:

- Vibrant colours such as orange and yellow to symbolise glowing health
- Bowls of fruit
- A diagram of the healthy food pyramid
- A book about nutrition
- Your promise to eat five helpings of fruit and vegetables, lean meat and fish, or whatever constitutes healthy eating for you

- Lots of affirmations
- Pictures showing people looking happy, healthy and fit
- Glowing, colourful pictures of fruit and vegetables
- A photo of you looking well and happy
- A sleek panther as your totem animal
- Add anything else you like – flowers, candles, incense, etc

Purify and re-dedicate your change-altar regularly. Spend some time there every day to reinforce your motivation and remind your unconscious of your intentions. Bring offerings and leave prayers, wishes and affirmations.

Celebrate your progress and give thanks for the changes you have already made. Use 'I summon the spirit of .... (whatever it is you want – serenity, wisdom, strength, clarity, warmth, health, grace, persistence, slenderness, sobriety, whatever) here now', as an affirmation along with your own personal ones.

Use longer periods at your altar for visualisation. Picture vividly how your life is changing and what your life will be like when you have achieved the change you want. Resolve at least one small step you'll take in the direction you want to go every time you perform an altar ritual.

Wishing well

This is a light-hearted altar dedicated to your wishes and dreams. Use either an attractive bowl or one of the many indoor fountains you can get now. Fill it with natural spring water (more evocative than tap water, even if you only get the bottled sort), and surround it with natural objects, such as stones, shells or plants. Add candles, woody incense, figures of woodland and water creatures, nature spirits, or anything else that makes it magical for you.

Use it like any other altar – bring flowers, light candles and spend time there. Write your wishes on slips of paper and leave them there. Use it like a proper wishing well too – grasp a coin in your hand, make your wish, visualise it strongly and drop the coin into the water.

Far from being an idle gesture, wishing and dreaming stimulates your imagination and opens your mind to possibilities. The more you use this sort of 'wish-craft', the more effective it becomes.

When the coins in the well start to build up, or when the well needs cleaning, remove the coins, wash and dry them and drop them in a charity collecting box. Clean and refill the well.

You can, of course, make a wishing well outside, if you want. Use an outdoor wall or pool fountain, garden pond, ceramic pot, or any other water feature that sparks your imagination.

An altar to your true self

This is a rather unusual altar and it can be a bit difficult to grasp initially. But if you try it and like it, it can have profound effects. This is an altar to the true you – the deep-down, authentic person you are underneath the roles we all play, the compromises we make, the masks we all wear. You find your real identity by getting to know what you truly want – what truly expresses *you*.

Start with an empty space – no candles, no flowers, nothing. Just sit with it for a little while every day, focusing on that empty space. Let one thing emerge that you want to put in that space. It might be a single orchid, it might be a photo of a parent, a child's toy, a simple crystal, anything. Accept it, whatever it is, and place it on your altar.

Spend time there every day, patiently letting the next thing you want to add rise to the surface. Keep going in this way and don't be concerned too much about the 'meaning' of the things you choose. Understanding tends to happen at an unconscious level long before it reaches the rational mind. Enlightenment will come in its own time.

Don't worry, either, if some of the things you choose seem to come from the dark side of your personality – we all have one.

Let the altar grow slowly, gradually letting a symbolic picture of your innermost being emerge.

Altars for celebration

You can also build altars to honour, commemorate and celebrate the things that are important in your life and beliefs, or that you would like to become more important.

Spiritual and religious beliefs

These are the classical altars everyone thinks of when you say the word 'altar'. An altar to your religious or spiritual beliefs is a physical expression of those beliefs and very personal to you. It can be extremely satisfying, though, to have a focal point for those thoughts and feelings.

Use it as a point of contact between your everyday life and the Divine. Pray and meditate there to unscramble your thoughts, calm your mind and listen to your inner self. It's a sacred place where you go to deepen your connection with the spirit.

What you put there is very much up to you, but it may help your sense of connection if you include:

- Something representing the Divine. A statue, picture or figure that symbolises the highest spiritual good to you. Established religions, ancient and modern, have clear symbols you could draw on, or you could decide on your own more personal representation.
- Something representing the blessings bestowed by the Divine. Choose something that reminds you of the generosity of the Divinity you have chosen. Flowers are

always good, but you might choose symbols of a rich harvest (sheaves of corn, grain, etc) if you chose the Earth Mother, or symbols of pity and compassion if your Divinity is a healer such as Jesus, Buddha, Kwan Yin. Some Divinities have many different blessings associated with them, choose the ones that have most relevance for you.

- Something that can carry your spirit to that higher place. Candles, crystals and mandalas are among the things used to attune the spirit to a higher realm. In other words, include something that makes you feel holy when you look at it!

An example of the above dedicated to Isis, the Egyptian Mother Goddess, might be:

- A statue of Isis to represent the Divine
- A bowl of fruit and flowers, and a figure of a mother and child to represent the blessings of fertility, regeneration and protection she brings
- A candle to uplift your spirit. (A crystal pyramid, too, would work well here)

Add anything else you like – pictures, poems, blessings, more candles, bells, symbols associated with your chosen Divinity, whatever.

Use the altar as you would any other. Purify and re-dedicate it regularly, spend a little time there every day with longer rituals when you have the time. Bring offerings and leave prayers, wishes and affirmations as you like.

Natural forces and elements

A variation on the spiritual or religious altar, these are dedicated not to divine spirits, but to natural forces. Use such an altar as a place of inspiration and renewal to recharge your spiritual batteries and remind you of the power of nature.

You could have an altar dedicated to:

- The four elements – Earth, Water, Fire and Air
- Any of the elements alone
- The four directions – North, South, East and West
- The Earth or personifications of the Earth such as Gaia
- The Sea or gods or goddesses of the Sea
- The Sun
- The Moon
- Rain, rainbows, thunder, lightning, wind, etc
- The Life Force
- Your zodiac sign, ruling planet, or Chinese astrological sign

The options are many and all of them intensely personal. Use your altar to express your beliefs physically – a focal point for your thoughts and feelings and a bridge between your everyday life and the forces of nature. Meditate there to deepen your sense of connection.

What you include depends on your personal views and your appreciation of these powers. But, as with the religious altar, it may help your sense of connection if you include:

- Something representing the Force of Power you are celebrating – a picture or object that symbolises it
- Something representing the blessings and benefits that power brings
- Something to lift your spirit to a higher level, such as candles, crystals or a mandala

For example, an altar dedicated to the Moon might be made up of white, blue and silver items and include:

- The figure of a lunar goddess or a round, silver mirror to represent the moon
- Tools for magic and divination to represent the blessings of intuition and enchantment the moon traditionally brings
- Silver candles to lift your spirit

You could also add white flowers, a white hare – traditional messenger between the moon and humankind, a moonstone, pictures of the moon over the sea to represent the sense of spiritual and physical tides, and anything else you like.

Ancestral altars

If your family and background are an important part of you or if, conversely, you feel you lack strong roots, you might like to honour who you are and where you came from with an ancestral altar.

Build it as you would any other altar and use it to honour your background, forebears, cultural heritage, family or cultural history, ethnic identity, or whatever else you value about your family or racial history.

Temporary altars

An altar doesn't have to be for ever. Make temporary ones to celebrate events and occasions. Spontaneous or planned, a special festive altar adds sparkle. Think about having:

- SEASONAL ALTARS - see Chapter Nine for celebratory ideas for the various festivals and holidays
- ACHIEVEMENT ALTARS - when you've achieved something important to you, give it due honour and celebration
- BIRTHDAY ALTARS – celebrate and affirm the one whose birthday it is. Include blessings and wishes for the coming year
- PARTY ALTARS – set the mood and express your hopes and desires for the occasion with a sparkling party altar

Chapter Five

Soul Food

Feed your soul

We all eat. So it's not surprising some of our oldest and most deeply ingrained rituals revolve around food.

What do we do when we want to celebrate? *Go for a meal.*

What do we do when we want to bond? *Go for a meal.*

What do we do when we want to get to know someone better? *Take them for a meal.*

How do we mark important occasions? *With a meal.*

How do we get friends and family together in one place? *By having a meal.*

How do we show we accept someone? *Invite them over for dinner.*

And when we do, we know, consciously or unconsciously, that we are nourishing a lot more than our bodies. We are aware we are taking something else into ourselves along with the food.

Something equally valuable to our wellbeing.

You are what you eat. Don't just wait for a special occasion. Add a little conscious ritual as one of the key ingredients to your everyday meals and you'll find you feed your mind, soul and spirit along with your body.

Making mealtimes special

We eat, on average, three times a day, seven days a week, three hundred and sixty-five days a year, and yet still manage to make some meals memorable. For such a basic, everyday thing, we certainly put a lot into it when we want to. Every major holiday has its special food associated with it. And it's not just full meals. What would weddings, birthdays or Christmas be without cake? Valentine's Day without chocolate?

It doesn't take extravagant amounts of time or money to turn mealtimes into nourishment for more than just the body, and ordinary food into soul food.

Choosing food

Choose your food to suit your mood – either the mood you're in or the mood you would like to be in. There are lots of different things you could base your choice on, or you could, literally, just follow your gut instinct.

Rainbow diet

Choose your food according to colour; pick the colour according to your needs. For added oomph use matching plates, flowers, candles and anything else you think of to set the table and get you in the right mood.

RED

Choose red for vitality. When you want a shot of energy, try a salad of red onion, red pepper, tomato, red radish and a dash of chilli. Follow up with a rare steak (for non-vegetarians, of course), or red lentils or chillied red kidney beans in a tomato-based sauce, and finish with strawberries and red currants. Play hot Latin music while you eat and see if you still feel tired afterwards.

PINK

Pink is the colour of love. A pink dinner *à deux* sets the scene beautifully. Try pink grapefruit or watermelon, pink salmon fillets with prawns, pink fir-apple potatoes and lollo rosso salad followed by raspberry mousse.

YELLOW AND ORANGE

Bring some sunshine into your life; choose yellow and orange foods when you need a lift. There are plenty of fruits and vegetables to choose from – yellow peppers, oranges, mangoes, peaches, carrots, pumpkin, lemons – prepare a golden salad to chase away the blues. How about a sunshine breakfast of scrambled eggs, golden cornflakes, apricots, peaches and honey? Accompany with the sunniest music you can find and a cup of lemon tea.

BROWN

Brown is grounding. When you feel up in the air or spaced out, bring yourself back down to earth with brown food and deep, rich flavours. Slowly cooked casseroles with rich gravy, baked potatoes, fresh brown bread, chocolate pudding and chocolate cake, for example.

GREEN

Let the balancing influence of nature get to work on you with green foods. When you feel stressed, have a day eating lots of green, leafy salads, herbs and vegetables and accompany each meal with soothing music and mint tea. Even better, get in touch with the natural world around you at the same time by eating in the garden, park or countryside.

BLUE AND PURPLE

The opposite of brown, blue and violet foods create a very spiritual and uplifting menu. Choose from the variety of purple fruits and berries available such as blueberries, damsons, plums, black grapes, blackberries and blackcurrants, as well as aubergines, purple broccoli, red cabbage and beetroot, mackerel, sardines and mussels.

White

Try white food when you feel over-stimulated and need a rest from everything. Ideally, treat yourself to a day in bed with an undemanding book or video and the simplest of comfort foods – milk, rice with chicken or white fish, mashed potatoes, vanilla ice cream or rice pudding. Unwind.

Rainbow drink

Try this when you could do with a bit of everything for maximum vitality and wellbeing. Pick a fruit for each colour of the rainbow – strawberry, orange, pineapple, kiwi, blueberry and black grape, for example. Extract the juice, and add to a base of apple juice. As you sip it slowly, visualise yourself filled with a rainbow light and surrounded with a rainbow aura.

(A small note of caution. None of the above are what you might call balanced diets. Don't stick to them for more than a day at a time at the most.)

Symbolically speaking

Choose your food for its symbolism and make mealtimes the opportunity for a mood-enhancing ritual.

- Need to keep your cool? Ice cream could be perfect, especially sharp, clear-headed lemon flavour. Or try a glacial meal of cold soup (gazpacho or vichyssoise), iceberg lettuce salad and lemon sorbet

- Share hot buttered toast with someone you need to 'butter up'
- Light, creamy foods are excellent when you need soothing and smoothing. Visualise them softening the rough corners as you eat
- Hand round chocolates or biscuits when the atmosphere needs sweetening
- Rich, rare and exotic foods could help when you're feeling poor and hard done by. Treat yourself to quails' eggs and a minute serving of caviar or half a dozen hand-made Belgian chocolates
- Fresh fruits and freshly squeezed juices will help you connect to living energy
- When you need to be bubbly, what could be better than a glass of champagne? Use lemonade for non-alcoholic occasions – it's the bubbles that are important, not the alcohol
- A spoonful or two of honey will remind you of your naturally sweet nature, or use it when you need a honeyed tongue to sweet-talk someone
- And if you need to spice up your life, you'll find lots of ideas below

Spice up your life

When your life needs added zing, try adding extra spice in the form of food. It will soon percolate through into the rest of your life. Add hot spices wherever you can:

- Mustard to hot dogs and hamburgers
- Chilli to soups and stews
- Curry spices to casseroles
- Nutmeg and cinnamon to cakes and puddings
- A pinch of ground ginger or cinnamon to coffee, or to the butter on buttered toast

As you eat or drink, imagine the spices filling you with warmth and vitality, or try the following specific recipes.

CHILLI WARMER

Chilli is fiery and vibrant, and so is paprika. Try these special spicy nuts to get you into a similar state.

Light a red candle and put some high-energy music on – salsa or something like that. Heat a little oil in a heavy pan and add about a half-teaspoon each of chilli powder and paprika. Add a spoonful of tomato puree to bind the spices together. Add a couple of handfuls of cashew nuts and stir-fry until thoroughly coated with the spicy mixture. Stir and shake the nuts in time to the music and, as you stir, visualise the mixture fizzing and spitting with energy. Imagine that energy being absorbed by the nuts.

Put the cashew nuts in a red bowl and sprinkle with a little sea-salt. As you eat them visualise drawing that fiery power into yourself. Imagine it releasing sparks of energy within you you didn't even know you had.

CINNAMON CAKE

Warmer, sweeter and more soothing than chilli, but still with an exotic touch, use cinnamon when you want rich, mellow feelings in your life. What could be more nurturing than baking a cake? Especially a cinnamon spice cake.

Cook by candlelight and play your favourite mood music. Warm the oven and line a cake tin with greaseproof paper or parchment. Put 300g of self-raising flour in a mixing bowl and add a teaspoon of ground cinnamon and a teaspoon of mixed spice. Stir the spice into the flour and visualise that rich, warm, exotic energy spreading throughout. Stir in a handful of dried fruit – currants, sultanas and/or raisins. Imagine the richness increasing. Add around 100g of the darkest, richest, softest brown sugar you can find. Stir, and visualise the mixture lush with the warm energy of cinnamon and spice. Stir the candle-light and the music into it, too.

Mix 300ml of milk with 4 tablespoons of oil and pour in. Beat until smooth and spoon into baking tin. Bake at 180°C / 350°F / Gas 4 for 40- 45 minutes.

(If you prefer to work with imperial measurements, use 12oz flour, 4oz of sugar and 12 fl oz of milk.)

While it bakes, concentrate on what's warm and mellow in your life. Write down what it is that makes you feel warm inside. Go through photo albums and keepsakes to remind you, if you like. Keep warm, loving thoughts in your mind while you smell the cinnamon and spice aroma.

Turn out and leave to cool.

Light a gold candle and eat a slice or two of cake slowly and lingeringly when you need cinnamon energy.

GINGER TEA

Need gingering up? The quickest way is ginger tea. Grate a thumb-sized chunk of ginger root into a zingy yellow or orange mug and pour on hot water. Add a teaspoon or two of honey, according to taste. Drink while visualising the fiery ginger energising every cell in your body and mind.

Preparing food

Preparing food is a kind of magic. It's an alchemy that can, if you want, add something amazing to food along with the physical ingredients. You can add good wishes, and positive intentions. It can even let you eat your words – in the best possible sense.

Mixing

Put your dreams and wishes into what you eat. When you stir anything – cake mix, scrambled eggs, batter, stir-fries, porridge, even your cup of tea or coffee, simply stir clockwise and visualise stirring in good wishes for love, happiness, success, tranquillity, or whatever else you want. Home-made bread is especially good for this – work your wishes energetically into the dough as you knead.

You can also add wishes along with all the other ingredients when you're making something like a casserole, fruitcake, or any other dish with lots of different things in it.

Use the following two rituals as examples and adapt them to your specific needs.

Stirring up love

Make yourself a love cake.

YOU WILL NEED:

>   Pink candles – from pale pink to deep crimson, depending on the degree of passion you want to awaken within yourself

>   As many varieties of dried fruit as you can find – currants, sultanas, dates, dried apricots, cherries, etc. Chop larger fruits into small pieces

>   Glass of red wine, or a non-alcoholic alternative such as red grape juice

>   Rich fruitcake recipe

Light the candles. Divide the fruits into separate piles. Name each with one of the blessings of love. You might choose romance, closeness, passion, friendship, companionship, shared laughter, whatever is important to you. Take time to linger over each fruit, visualising the individual blessing. Take a sip of the red wine and make a toast to love. Gently warm the remainder in a saucepan (don't let the wine boil). Add the fruits, visualising pouring in love. Stir gently, stirring all your loving feelings into the mixture. Leave to cool, letting the fruit absorb the wine. Continue, using your favourite cake recipe. As you stir the cake mix, don't forget to picture stirring in love and blessings.

Eat the cake by candlelight with a glass of the red wine, or a non-alcoholic alternative, such as spring water or fruit juice. Invite someone special over to share it.

Bird cake

Feed your troubles to the birds.

YOU WILL NEED:

Unsalted nuts and seeds – sunflower seeds,
  pumpkin seeds, etc

Lard, dripping or other natural fat

Yoghurt pot

String

Put the nuts and the seeds in separate piles. Name each little heap with one of your worries or problems. Melt the fat in a saucepan and pour in the nuts and seeds. Visualise pouring in all your problems. Stir vigorously, beating all your ill feeling into the mixture.

Pour the mixture into a yoghurt pot or something similar and leave to cool. Ease out of the pot when cold, thread a string through the middle and hang it up outside. Watch in great satisfaction over the next few days as the birds enjoy your offering and your troubles melt away along with the nuts and seeds.

Processing

There are simple but satisfying rituals to be got out of the most basic things. Processing food is one of them.

Blender magic

When things need smoothing over, try a bit of blender magic and make a soothing soup.

YOU WILL NEED:

A selection of your favourite vegetables

Vegetable stock or something similar

Blender

Name the vegetables for the people or things that need soothing or unifying. Take a few moments to visualise them clearly. Cook the vegetables in the stock until soft. Imagine the people, attitudes or problems softening along with them.

Blend together with strong a visualisation of unity and wholeness. Drink the soup, enjoying its smooth creaminess and picturing clearly how such different elements have blended together so effortlessly. If other people are involved, invite them along to enjoy it too.

Drip-filter

Sometimes you know you're capable of doing something, you just can't quite get it together. All that potential seems locked up inside you waiting to be released. Next time you make coffee with a drip filter, add some spiritual energy to the brew along with the usual caffeine.

YOU WILL NEED:

Ground coffee

Coffee maker

Pen and paper

Fill the filter with ground coffee and smell the delicious aroma. This is going to be a great cup of coffee, but it needs something to happen to it first. All that potential is locked up in the coffee grounds, waiting to be released. As you sit and watch the coffee drip through, feel the potential begin to be released in you also. Drop by drop, the possibilities within you are materialising.

Drink the coffee slowly. As you do, jot down any ideas that occur to you. Include at least one specific step, however small, you could do next.

Juice extractor

Rely on juicers to extract the essence out of anything.

When you feel confused or troubled about something, take a couple of pieces of fruit to represent the problem. Drop them in the extractor and watch the juice pouring out clear and sweet. Clear out the soggy, discarded pulp and throw it in the bin or on the compost heap with great satisfaction. Drink the juice and picture your mind, too, becoming free of clogging mush.

Water purifier

Do you need to be clear about something? Do you feel other stuff keeps getting in the way, clouding the issue? Try this simple water-filter ritual.

YOU WILL NEED:

Water filter

Water

Glass jug and wineglass

Take the jug of unfiltered water. Stare into it and visualise it murky with the problems clouding you. Project all your uncertainty and doubt into it. Pour the water into the filter and let it work its way through. Picture all the negativity being drawn out of it. As each fresh drop drips through, notice its sparkling clarity.

Pour the filtered water into the wineglass and sip it slowly. Let that same cool clarity flow into every cell of your body and every thought in your head. By the end of the glass you should feel much clearer in your own mind.

Cooking

You can even add symbolism to your food along with the way you cook it. Pick a cooking method that suits your spiritual needs.

Oven

The oven has long been a symbol of warmth and nurturing. When you want more of these things in your life, bake some into a loaf of bread or a cake.

YOU WILL NEED:

Candles

Bread or cake recipe or packet mix or part-baked product

Oven

Work by candlelight. Make up the loaf or cake and put into a pre-heated oven. While it bakes concentrate on what it is that needs more warmth and nurturing. Look at photos, write down ideas, go through keepsakes and albums, whatever feels right. Keep warm, loving thoughts in your mind while you do so. Imagine your loaf or cake basking in the heat of love, the warmth baking it and transforming it from cold, inert dough into something warm, nourishing and delicious.

Curl up and relax as you enjoy the bread or cake. Share it with someone special if you like.

Microwave

When you cook with a microwave, you are literally adding energy to your food. When you need more zeal and enthusiasm, choose something to eat you can zap in the microwave first. Visualise all that energy perking you up along with the food.

Stir fry

Another energy fixer. Cook quickly on a high heat and stir with vigour. Visualise adding real zest to your meal as you swirl it round the pan. For even greater effect, use red, orange and yellow foods and add lots of hot spices.

Casserole

Casseroling represents a slow blending together over time. The sum of the parts are greater than the whole. Use a casserole symbolically to bring a group together.

YOU WILL NEED:

A group of people you want to bring together. Ask each one to bring a different ingredient to go into the pot – vegetables, herbs and spices, meat or fish, beans or lentils, etc

Casserole basics such as salt, stock, flour for thickening, flavourings, etc

Big spoon for stirring

Foolproof casserole recipe

Casserole pot

Start the casserole off and ask everyone to add their own contribution. Make any adjustments for seasoning, liquid, etc. Let everyone give it a good stir with the spoon, adding their good wishes as they do so. Leave the casserole to cook itself while you enjoy each other's company. When it's ready, ladle out the food and enjoy a meal together as a group along with bread, wine and whatever else you fancy.

You can also use a casserole to unify different parts of your own life that don't seem to be getting on too well – home and work, for example. Pick ingredients to represent the different things that need bringing together. Make the casserole as above. While it's cooking, write down ideas that might help you balance the elements in your life. As you eat the casserole, enjoy the blending of flavours and ingredients and visualise everything in your life combining as easily and with such delicious effect.

Decorating

Have you ever tried eating your words? We do it every time we put a greeting on a birthday, wedding or Christmas cake. Why not extent the ritual to everyday foods and wish yourself happiness and luck all the time. Imagine the words becoming a part of you as you eat them.

- Pipe good wishes in icing on cakes and biscuits

- Paint them on with food colouring and a small brush
- Remember conversation hearts, little sweets with words and phrases such as 'Be mine' and 'Love' written on them? Use the idea to decorate little sweets or biscuits with the sentiments you prefer. How about 'Go for it' and 'Simply the best' when you need motivation?
- Sprinkle symbols in sugar on top of cakes, pies and tarts, even on your morning cereal or oatmeal – hearts for love, stars so you shine, pound signs to feel rich, a crescent moon to remind you of your intuition, and so on
- Do the same with a drizzle of honey
- Carve words, wishes or symbols into the butter or spread on a piece of bread or toast

Freezing

Use your freezer to put your problems on ice for a bit, or take the heat out of a situation.

YOU WILL NEED:

Pen and paper

Freezer bag

Water in a freezer-proof bowl

Freezer

Focus on the problem and write it down on the piece of paper. Fold or roll it up tightly. Wrap it in the freezer bag and put it in a bowl of water in the freezer. Visualise it slowly freezing and sense the urgency of the problem gradually cooling down. Leave it there for as long as necessary.

When you have more time or resources to look at the problem, take it out of the freezer. As it thaws, visualise the problem itself becoming softer and more malleable. Take another sheet of paper and jot down any ideas that come to you. Try to put down at least one step you could take towards a solution.

Either put the paper back into the freezer until you're ready to take further steps, or, if you feel the problem is resolved, bury it in the garden to rot away naturally.

Complete meals for the soul

Obviously, you're not going to the following lengths if you're just making a sandwich or grabbing a quick breakfast. Sometimes, though, it's fun to prepare a complete ritual meal, either for your own enjoyment or to share with others.

Don't just save it just for birthdays and holidays. Why not restore traditional ritual meals such as Sunday lunch for family or friends, or invent new ones such as after-work dinners on Fridays, or everyone-bring-a-dish lunches on Wednesdays? One place I know has an office breakfast with fresh-baked croissants every Friday morning.

Add a little ritual and you could have a regular soul-reviver.

Preparing ritual meals needn't involve complicated or expensive recipes, it's the spiritual dimension that counts, and you can add that to anything. You can even use ready-made food if you just follow some simple ideas to transform it into soul food.

- CHOOSE YOUR FOOD WITH CARE. Pick what's appropriate for the purpose you have in mind. A meal to enhance love and passion, for example, would be unlikely to feature hamburger and chips. (Unless they're a treasured reminder of your first evening together, of course.) Consider growing your own food, too. Even herbs from a window box or salad from a patio pot have something special about them when you've grown them yourself.

- TAKE YOUR TIME preparing the meal. Light candles and play music to put you in a ritual frame of mind while you work. Visualise the purpose of your ritual meal. Hold your hands over the ingredients and bless them with the qualities you desire – love, peace, joy, wisdom, etc.

- KEEP YOUR PURPOSE IN MIND as you prepare the food. Even if you are using ready-made meals, add something of your own you can endow with love and care. Chop some herbs to sprinkle over dishes, grate fresh parmesan, add icing and sugar strands to cakes or biscuits, grate chocolate over cheesecake, chop fruit and add with a sprig of mint to lemonade, for example.

- PUT YOUR WISHING IN THE MIXING. Mix your wishes and dreams into the food as you chop, sprinkle and stir.

- MAKE THE MOST OF SYMBOLISM. It's what your unconscious mind responds to, so the way you prepare food as well as what you choose is important. A tricky dinner with in-laws? Get the blender working to produce smooth, soothing soups and mousses. Want the evening to go with a zing? Make some popcorn in the microwave and get things buzzing.

- MAKE THE TABLE SPECIAL. Look at a table set for a celebration dinner. It has candles, flowers, special vessels ... yes, it's an altar! Treat your table just as you would a shrine. Choose a special cloth and add flowers, candles and other symbolic decorations. You could even include photos, wishes and affirmations tucked in among the plates and napkins – they make a great talking point during the meal.
- SAY GRACE or a blessing before the meal, if that's your style. If not, offer a toast before you begin. Either way, you get to subtly state your intention for this ritual meal.
- EAT WITH PURPOSE. Visualise all those wishes and intentions you put into the food entering your body and becoming a part of you with every mouthful.
- TAKE YOUR TIME over the meal, just as you did over the preparation. If you're in company, enjoy the conversation and the sense of sharing a special occasion. Even when you're alone, don't rush to get up from the table. Relax and enjoy the atmosphere you've created.
- IF YOU WANT TO CONTINUE your ritual and include the washing up, see *Dish the Dirt* in Chapter Two for ideas.

Try any of the following rituals that appeal to you. Accompany them with visualisation, good wishes and blessings.

Sunshine breakfast

Treat yourself to something special at weekend or holiday breakfasts when you don't have to rush off anywhere. Invite some healing and cheering solar energy into your life.

YOU WILL NEED:

Sun-coloured flowers

Yellow, orange or gold cloth

Yellow, orange or gold plates and dishes where possible

Sun-coloured food such as golden fruits, toast, marmalade, cereals

Choose a sunny day and sit in the sun to eat, either outside or at a window. Set the table with a sun-coloured cloth, bright flowers – yellows and oranges – and any other sun symbols you might have. As you prepare your breakfast and eat it, focus on absorbing the sun's energy and incorporating it into your food.

- Be aware of the sun on your skin and the shimmer and glint of light over the table

- Drizzle a sun symbol in honey (a circle with spreading rays) over your breakfast cereal

- Select golden fruits, such as peaches and apricots, and visualise the fruit growing and ripening in the sun. Imagine you still sense that dazzling energy radiating from the fruit

- As you toast bread, visualise the heat of the sun warming it and turning it golden

- If you're eating cereal or bread, picture the grains developing and ripening like living gold in the sunshine

- Inscribe a sun symbol in the butter on your toast

- If you drink fruit juice, hold the glass it up to the light and visualise it absorbing the colour and energy of the sun

- Let the light flow into you. Think about the power of the sun, the source of all life, and imagine it pouring into you

- Imagine you are eating and drinking pure sunlight. Feel that glorious radiance become a part of you

Picnic power

Take a picnic out into the countryside for a healing, restoring, re-balancing meal. If you can't get to the country, a park or garden will work just as well. Find yourself a secluded, tranquil spot.

YOU WILL NEED:

Picnic basket and cloth

Natural foods – leafy green salad, nuts and fruits, lots of herbs for flavouring

Fruit juices or herb teas to drink

Bird cake – see earlier in this chapter, or some bread crumbs

Wear comfortable shoes and clothes you can relax in. If possible, stroll to your picnic spot rather than driving. If you do drive, still have a short walk before you eat to stimulate your appetite. Enjoy the natural world around you – drink in the sunshine, green grass, rustling trees, birdsong and butterflies. Sit where you can enjoy sunshine and shade, and spread out your picnic. As you enjoy your meal, focus on absorbing the gentle, green power of nature. Let it soothe and relax you.

- Take time to eat. Relax completely before you start

- Be aware of where you are. Feel the earth solidly beneath you, the sky above you and the abundance of life around you

- If you like, pick some simple wild flowers – daisies, dandelions or buttercups to decorate your 'table'

- Select fresh, green foods such as lettuce and cucumber and visualise it glowing with life. Imagine you can actually see a gentle, green, healing energy radiating from it

- Smell the scent of grass, flowers and leaves around you

- Take time to enjoy the similar fresh scent of the food you are eating

- Hold a glass of fruit juice and visualise it absorbing the colour and energy of the green world around you. Let it flow into you as you drink it

- After you've eaten, sit or even lie down quietly and absorb the energy around you Breathe it in, drawing it into yourself, and visualise it soothing and healing every cell in your body

- Hang up the bird cake, if you've made some, or name the bread crumbs with your worries and scatter them for the birds to enjoy

- Tidy up and leave feeling renewed and refreshed. Leave all your troubles behind for the birds

Moon meal

Try this special meal to stimulate your intuitive side and add some mystery and magic to your life.

YOU WILL NEED:

Pale blue, pale lilac and white flowers – scented ones like jasmine and white roses are particularly lovely

Silver or white cloth

Silver, white or pale blue plates and dishes where possible

Moon-pale food such as rice, dairy food, white fish, white wine, and pale fruits such as lychees

Choose the evening of a full moon, if you can, and eat where you'll see it – either outside or at a window. Set the table with a moon-coloured cloth, white and silver candles, pale flowers, and any other moon symbols you might have. As you prepare and eat your meal, concentrate on absorbing and assimilating the moon's energy into your food.

- Eat by candlelight and enjoy the soft glow of light over the table

- Fill a shallow glass or silver bowl with water. Float candles and white petals on it to reflect the moon

- Make little cakes or biscuits and sprinkle a lunar crescent symbol in white sugar on them or pipe it in white icing

- Pour a glass of spring water, add a moonstone or quartz

crystal and leave it where it catches the moon's rays. Visualise the crystal drawing down the moonlight and filling the glass with the essence of lunar magic. Drink it slowly

- Select white fish and pale fruits. Picture shoals of silver fish in the moonlit water, and sense the gentle tidal pull of the moon. Visualise the moon gently drawing water up from deep inside the earth, into the plants and into the fruits. Sense it pulling at your own internal tides

- Take a glass of white wine, or light-coloured fruit juice. Hold it up to the light and visualise it absorbing the silvery light of the moon

- Sip it and let the light flow into you. Visualise yourself being filled with that mysterious silver radiance. Hold the glass in your hands and gaze down into it, picturing the moon cradled there. Imagine yourself cloaked in moonlight, crowned with a silver crescent. Feel that radiance become a part of you

- Drink jasmine tea to finish

Rainbow blessings

Try this for a special breakfast or lunch. Use it to bring colour and joy into your life, and to give you the opportunity to count your blessings and open your unconscious mind to receiving more of them.

YOU WILL NEED:

Flowers in a rainbow of bright colours

Rainbow-patterned or brightly coloured table cloth

Plates and dishes of as many different colours as possible

Brightly coloured fruits and vegetables – oranges, apricots, blueberries, bananas, strawberries, tomatoes, peppers, etc

Rainbow drink – see page 127

Pen and paper

Sit in the sun to eat, and hang cut-glass crystals where they catch the light and create rainbow reflections to dance over the table. Set the table with as many different colours as possible – cloth, flowers, crockery, bowls of fruit, etc. Drape the table with rainbow ribbons in your favourite colours. Add any rainbow symbols you might have and any other brightly coloured things as well as anything that makes you happy to look at it. Play your favourite upbeat music.

During the meal, focus on absorbing all the colour around you.

- Enjoy the shimmer and glint of rainbows as they sparkle over the table

- Pour a glass of spring water and leave it where it will catch some of the rainbow light. Visualise light filling the glass with brilliant colour, laughter and joy. At the end of the meal, sip it slowly and with pleasure

- Try rainbow stripes of strawberry, orange, gooseberry and blackcurrant jam on a piece of toast

- Enjoy rainbow-coloured fruits and vegetables – as many different colours as you can find. See if you can sense the different energy of each different colour as you eat

- As you eat and drink, use the pen and paper to write down all the joys and pleasures in your life – everything that makes you happy, all your favourite things. Take your time and enjoy it

- Take the glass of Rainbow Drink and hold it in your hands. Visualise it absorbing all the dancing rainbow rays surrounding you. Imagine you actually sense that dazzling energy within the fruit juice

- Sip it and let those rainbows flow into you. Visualise yourself being filled with colour and laughter. Imagine yourself clothed in rainbows, crowned with a coronet of bright flowers. Feel all those glorious colours become a part of you

- When you've finished, roll your list up, tie it with some of the ribbons and tuck a flower or two in for luck. Put it where you will see it to remind you of your joy

Little rituals

WHEN EVERYTHING SEEMS SOUR, make some lemonade and see if it sweetens things up. Squeeze the juice from a couple of lemons, but don't add any sugar yet. Taste the unsweetened juice. It will probably be almost unbearable. Focus on the bitterness, and associate it in your mind with the sourness of your situation. Add a small amount of sugar and taste it again. Focus on detecting even the slightest improvement. Add more sugar and taste again. Continue with this and gradually, almost imperceptibly, the lemon juice will become sweet and palatable. As will your problem. Keep sipping sweet lemonade at regular intervals to remind you of this until you have resolved the difficulty.

WHEN EVERYTHING SEEMS DARK and impenetrable, try a simple coffee ritual to lighten things up. Make some strong, black coffee. Stare into it and see the blackness that surrounds you. Add some milk or cream. Notice how even the smallest drop has an effect, making the coffee a deep, rich brown rather than impenetrable black. Add some more. Keep going until you have a cup of light, creamy coffee. There is light at the end of the tunnel.

WHEN YOU'RE FACED WITH SOMETHING UNPALATABLE, try some chocolate magic to make it easier to swallow. Get a large chunk of stale, dry (but still edible) white bread. Name it with your problem and visualise your difficulties embodied in it – stale, dry and hard to swallow. Melt some chocolate in a small bowl over hot water. Tear small pieces off the bread, dip them in the chocolate and eat. As you do, visualise treating your difficulty in the same way – breaking it down into small, bite-size pieces. Enjoy the taste of the chocolate as you work your way right through the problem.

Chapter Six

Personal Magic

Release your soul

As the song says, you've got to 'eliminate the negative and accentuate the positive' if you want your soul to grow and thrive. This chapter looks at personal wellbeing and includes rituals designed to clear negativity from the mind and spirit and replace it with positive energy. They can also be used to enhance motivation, creating change and fulfilment at deep levels.

Use these personal rituals to:

- Release negativity, unwanted habits and addictions
- Find your goals in life
- Protect yourself from negativity
- Achieve personal change
- Attain desired qualities

Releasing Negativity

Your soul can't thrive on negativity. When you are preoccupied with negative thoughts about yourself, your problems or the world around you it's virtually impossible to be open to any positive messages trying to get through. It's all too easy, though, to fall into the habit of listening to the inner critic, the inner cynic or the inner prophet of doom. Use these rituals to help erase negativity gently, but firmly and decisively.

Mind changer

Banish negative thoughts and beliefs about yourself with this ritual designed to encourage a more positive attitude.

YOU WILL NEED:

Paper and pen

Candle and something to inscribe it with

Piece of dark fabric (roughly handkerchief size)

Small box

Inscribe the rune of happiness, Wynn ᚹ , on the candle and light it. Think about your negative beliefs and pick one that's currently a problem for you. Tackle one area at a time. Don't try to confront every negative thought you have about yourself at once. Write down that negative belief on a piece of paper. Roll it up, wrap it in the fabric and put it in the box. Put the box in a safe place out of sight.

Take another sheet of paper and write down the opposite of your negative thought. If, for example, you wrote, 'I'm slow, stupid and useless at everything', you need to put, 'I'm quick, intelligent and good at everything.' 'I'm fat and lazy', becomes, 'I'm thin and energetic.' Look at this new statement about yourself and, underneath, write your reaction to it. Usual ones include, 'Ha ha ha', 'Rubbish', and 'No I'm not'.

Write down the statement again. Look at it and make your response. Keep doing this until you've written the new statement at least ten times. You'll find your responses change as you keep repeating the statement. You could, perhaps, find yourself writing at length about past experiences or how you feel. You could also find your attitude shifting slightly – 'No I'm not', becoming, 'I could be, maybe', and then, 'I am, sometimes.' Keep the paper somewhere safe.

Repeat the ritual regularly, once a week, say. After a couple of months, take the original negative statement out of its box. If you feel it no longer applies to you and you're ready to leave it behind, burn it and bury the ashes. If not, put it away and continue with the ritual until you are ready.

Bye-bye beans

Keep your outlook positive with this little ritual to nip bad thoughts in the bud.

YOU WILL NEED:

A packet of bean seeds (broad beans are the biggest)

A small pouch or envelope to keep them in

Carry the beans with you in a bag or pocket. When a negative thought strikes, take out a bean and whisper the thought into it. Hold it in your hand for a moment, visualising it absorbing the negativity along with the whispered thought. Hurl it as far away from you as you can with a firm and, if possible, cheerful 'Good-bye', either out loud or silently.

In quiet moments, picture the beans sprouting and growing, transforming your negative thoughts into healthy green plants with plenty of new young beans to feed the birds and squirrels.

Fan mail

Try the following bit of nonsense to boost your self-esteem. It sounds totally daft, but it works surprisingly well.

YOU WILL NEED:

A page in your diary or somewhere else private

Pen with gold ink

At the top of the page in big letters write: 'We think (your name) is wonderful. Signed ...' Underneath, write the names of every single person you admire. Every pop star, rock star and film star you've ever had a crush on, everyone you've ever fancied, still fancy, or might fancy in future. Every friend, relative, next-door-neighbour, nieces and nephews, your boss ... Interestingly, you may find you have to push through a surprising amount of resistance to write some of those names down.

Keep the list going. Whenever you think of someone new, or meet someone, add their name to it.

Feather light

Try *Blow away blues* (see page 25) to dispel a negative mood or do the following simple ritual.

YOU WILL NEED:

A bunch of feathers

A blue ribbon

Tie the feathers into a bunch with the ribbon. Hold them up to the sun (or the sky if there's no sun) and imagine them becoming light and airborne, floating with an airy grace. Picture them absorbing sunlight and moonlight and starlight as they float higher and higher.

Gently brush the feathers through the air around your head and face and down over your body as if you were using a feather duster. Sense them brushing away all the negativity surrounding you. Imagine them actually tickling your aura, especially when they get to the stomach area.

Believe me, it's very hard keeping a straight face doing this, never mind a sour mood.

Beautiful blue balloons

Let go of your problems and watch them just float away with this light-hearted ritual.

YOU WILL NEED:

A blue balloon for each of your problems

Marker pen

An open place out of doors

Go to an open place on a breezy day. Blow up the balloons and write a problem on each of them. How many you have is up to you, one may be enough, or you may want several. Hold the balloon in your hand and visualise it drifting up, up and away, taking your problem with it. Open your eyes and release the balloon. Repeat for each of your problems.

Off with the old, on with the new

When you need to change your luck, your mind or your attitude, try this traditional ritual for casting off the old and getting on with the new.

YOU WILL NEED:

A new item of clothing

An old item of clothing you can afford to throw away (an old shirt would do)

A wastepaper bin

A bath

Sea salt

Candles

Put on the old piece of clothing. Light the candles and run a bath. Pour in a handful of salt. Take off the old clothes. Visualise shucking off your old skin and your old luck along with the clothing. Drop them in the bin. Get into the bath. Soak and relax in the candlelight for as long as you want. Visualise the salt water drawing out any lingering negativity within you and dissolving it completely away.

Get out of the bath, dry off, and dress in your new, fresh clothes. Imagine putting on a new, fresh future along with them.

Let the water out and picture the last of the old, dark negativity going down the plughole with it. Bundle up the old clothes and throw them away.

Habit Breakers

Habits and addictions are a very specific form of negative thought and behaviour. Breaking them takes a lot of optimism, will-power and determination along with an unshakeable faith in a positive outcome. Use rituals to help you break their grip and support you along the way.

Turn back the clock

Have you ever wished you'd never started something –
smoking, gambling, a destructive relationship, for example?
This ritual (along with a lot of will-power, courage and
support) can help you turn the clock back and start afresh.

YOU WILL NEED:

A mirror

A clock, preferably with a second hand

*A symbol of what you want to change – maybe a
cigarette, a betting slip, a photo of the person
concerned or a picture representing the situation
you're in*

Two candles

Red wax crayon or marker pen

Piece of paper

Put the mirror upright in front of you and prop the clock up so
you see it reflected in the mirror. Inscribe one candle with the
rune of strength, Ur ♫, and the other with the rune for choice,
Peorth ᚲ, and put one each side of the mirror. Light the
candles. Put your symbol in front of you so it too is reflected in
the mirror. (This may take a bit of juggling, but take the time
to get it right.)

Looking only at the reflection, contemplate the symbol – what
it means to you and the burden it has become. Still looking
only in the mirror, take the pen or crayon and mark a big red
'X' over the reflection. Gaze at that red 'X' and visualise being

able to refuse your habit. See yourself clearly refusing whatever it is you're addicted to.

Turn your attention to the reflected clock. Watch it running backward (this will be especially clear if it has a second hand) and begin to visualise your life running backwards, too. Think about the last time you indulged in your unwanted habit, go back to the time before that, and the time before that until you arrive back at the first time you can remember.

Close your eyes and visualise saying 'No' at that point. Rewrite the scene so you happily decide to refuse and walk away. Replay the scene several times in your mind, each time making the choice to say 'No' and walk away. Clearly visualise your life taking a different path from that point of saying 'No'. Revisit each memory and change it to a different, positive one until you come back to the present day.

Mark a piece of paper with another big red 'X', and use it to wrap up your symbol. Stare hard at that 'X' and again picture yourself refusing to indulge. You have rewritten the past and the future will automatically be different.

Finish the ritual and snuff the candles. Put your wrapped symbol where you can see it and keep it there for the next week. Then, either bury or burn it or, if that's not possible, put it at the back of a drawer or cupboard, out of reach.

Rip it up

Keep your resolve going with this simple ritual two or three times a day.

YOU WILL NEED:

Paper

Pen – a big red marker pen is very useful

It's a good idea to keep a pad of paper and a pen especially for this. Design a symbol for the habit you are banishing, something you can draw quickly and easily – the outline of a cigarette, the outline of a cake, a teardrop for an unhappy relationship, for example.

Draw the symbol big and bold on the paper. Stare at it and summon up all your anger at having let it control you up to now. Rip the paper into tiny pieces and let your anger out.

Demons out

Cravings can sneak up on you at the most unexpected times. When they do, always have something lined up to distract you – decide what works well for you and make a list so you have help ready when temptation strikes. (You really do need a list, there's nothing like temptation to make you 'forget' your plans.) Use this ritual at the same time to back up your good intentions.

YOU WILL NEED:

Just yourself

Visualise the craving as a black, toxic cloud inside you. It could be in your chest, your head or your stomach. Different people feel it in different places. Take a deep breath and imagine the new breath swirling through that dark cloud, breaking it up and dissolving it. Pull the breath right into the centre of it. Blow the breath out forcefully (as though blowing out a particularly stubborn candle) and picture blowing the poisonous cloud out with it. (Stop and take a few normal breaths if you start to feel giddy.) Do this a few times until you dispel the black cloud, then go on with your planned diversion.

Goodbye to all that

Have you ever been stuck in this situation: you've made some changes for the better and you should be racing ahead with your life but somehow the past still keeps clinging on and holding you back? Maybe you've been promoted but feel like a fraud, or you've lost weight but still feel fat; you've stopped smoking but still hanker after a cigarette, or you've left a bad relationship but wonder if you did the right thing? Leave the past behind you and welcome the future with this ritual.

YOU WILL NEED:

Something that symbolises the part of the past you want to leave behind

Something that symbolises the part of the past you want to take with you into the future

Something that symbolises the future you want

(For these symbols, you may have some suitable

*object, picture or photograph, or you may like to
write something down on paper that sums up the
situation for you)*

Two red candles

A toothpick or something similar

A scarf in your favourite colour

Fireproof container

In your mind, divide the room where you are into two – one
half to represent the past and the other half to represent the
future. Put your symbol of the future in the 'future' half of the
room. Put the two symbols of the past in the 'past' half, along
with the scarf. Inscribe the rune of beginning, Beorc ᛒ , on
both candles and light them. Place them in the middle of the
room so you will pass between them when you go from one
half of the room to the other.

Sit with your symbols of the past. Take some time to think
back over what has happened and how you feel about it. Take
the symbol for the part of the past you want to leave behind.
Reflect on it and say a final goodbye. If possible (if it's a photo
or written statement, for example), light it in one of the
candle flames and let it burn away to ash in the fireproof
container. (Please be very, very careful.) If not, either crumple
it up or push it firmly away from you with the resolve to bury
it, throw it away or give it away as soon as possible.

Take the other symbol – what you want to take with you into
the future – and think about it for a while. What are you
taking with you from the past into the future? Courage,
maybe, or determination or the strength to change. Wrap it
carefully in the scarf while you say to yourself, 'The past is

over and gone, the future is waiting for me.'

Walk between the candles into the half of the room that represents your future. In ancient Celtic ritual, passing through fire represented the transition from one life to another.

Pick up the symbol of your future and spend some time thinking about it while the candles burn down a little. Unwrap the other symbol from your scarf and put the two together somewhere where you will see them frequently over the coming days. Wrap the scarf around your neck. Wear it every day for the next week and often, thereafter, for the next couple of months. Don't forget to snuff the candles when you've finished.

Attach Your Soul to Your Goal

Take your aspirations seriously. When you have goals, projects, dreams and ventures they're worth building altars to, doing rituals for, and anything else to integrate them firmly into your unconscious. A burning ambition so easily dwindles to an idle daydream in the hustle and bustle of everyday life. (Did I have an altar and ritual to get this book done? Of course I did. Otherwise it would have remained just another of the many things I intend to get around to 'some day'.) Attach your soul to your dreams with these rituals.

FileOfun

When you have a particular goal you want to achieve, it's important to keep your unconscious mind sensitised to it. One way of doing this is to keep a special file especially for that and nothing else. Invest it with a touch of ritual to make it even more special.

YOU WILL NEED:

A box file or file-folder

Gold ribbon or cord

Paper and pen with gold ink

Gold candles

Either find a file you like the look of, or cover one especially with attractive paper or fabric (gold or a vivid orange or flame colour would be a good choice). Collect together any information, pictures, leaflets, and such like that you already have. Light the candles.

Think about your goal. Dream about it and visualise achieving it. See yourself taking the steps you need to take, overcoming obstacles, being resourceful and inventive, enjoying victory. In gold ink, write down your intention, 'I ...... (your name) will ....'. Go on to define, as clearly and in as much detail as you can, exactly what your goal is. Put your statement, along with anything else you have, into the file and tie the gold ribbon or cord around it.

Keep a lookout for anything related to your goal. Jot down any thought and ideas you have, and keep them in a safe place. Put in your file:

- Specific information related to your goal
- The practical steps you need to take, as and when you think of them
- Related ideas and information
- Pictures and images that represent your goal
- Success stories of people in similar situations
- Inspiring quotes
- Supportive affirmations

Once a week, light the candles and open up your file. Re-read your goal statement first, then look through your collection and absorb the positive images and information. Add at least one practical thing, however small, that you will do over the coming week. Write it down in gold ink and add it to the file along with any new material you have collected. Close your file and re-tie the gold ribbon.

Word of encouragement

What if you don't have a goal? What if life is just one big rut and you can't think of anything, short of a miracle, that would make it any more exciting? What you need is a ritual to invoke random inspiration.

YOU WILL NEED:

Photo of you as a child (or, if you don't have one, a picture recalling your childhood)

Large piece of paper

Pen

Any book that has a strong emotional meaning for you (poetry book, childhood favourite, religious text, or something similar)

Candle

Inscribe the candle with the rune of attunement, Lagu ↑ , and light it. Gaze at the picture of yourself as a child and let your mind drift back to that time. Let your thoughts wander over what you were like back then. What did you enjoy? What were your favourite things? Who were your friends and what games did you play? What were your favourite subjects at school, your favourite television programmes? What hobbies and pastimes absorbed your interest?

Take the book and open it anywhere. Close your eyes and let your finger pick a word at random. (If it's something like 'and', 'the', or 'but', pick the next usable word on the same line.) Write this word in big letters in the middle of the sheet of paper. Draw a line out from the central word and, at the end of it, write down the first word your mind associates with it. If any associations with this new word occur to you, draw lines out from this word and jot your ideas down. When you run out of associations, go back to your central word, draw a line and start again. Do this over and over. Keep going until lines and words radiate out from your central word like the branches of a tree and the page is full.

Somewhere in that branching tree of words is the key to your needs and desires. Your unconscious mind will always try to bend random associations round to its own interests. It may be clearly apparent as you look at it. Maybe you became involved and energised as you followed a chain of ideas; maybe some recurring thread keeps appearing. Write down an outline of what it is.

If it isn't clear, put the paper away for a couple of days. When you look at it again, something you were too close to see before will almost invariably stand out.

Let the ideas mull over in your mind for the next few days. Visualise them as seeds germinating in the fertile warmth of your imagination. At the end of this time a clear sense of your direction should begin to emerge. As soon as you have a definite goal in mind, write it down.

Power project

It's nice to have a ritual to mark the beginning of a new project or enterprise. It gives it a positive start rather than just drifting into it. It's also great for building a sense of common purpose if there are several of you involved.

YOU WILL NEED:

A table for an altar

A symbol of the project

All the good luck charms you can lay your hands on

Flowers and candles to decorate the altar

Pen and several pieces of paper

Food and drink for celebration

If possible, get everyone involved in the new project together, but it will work just as well if it's just something personal to you. The point of the ritual is to build confidence and enthusiasm so the project will get off to a good start.

You don't have to make a big thing in front of other people about having an altar if you don't want to, it's just a focal point where you put things, but make it as festive as you can, with lots of colour. A colourful cloth, flowers, ribbons and streamers, candles ... you could ever scatter flower petals, glitter, sequins, stars or confetti around to add to the party mood. Include music too, rituals don't have to be carried out in an atmosphere of solemn silence.

Put the symbol for your project in the centre and surround it with good luck symbols. You could include lucky black cats, a new moon, a laughing Buddha, a chimney sweep, four-leaf clovers, horseshoes or any other traditional bringers of good fortune – real objects, pictures or photographs. Lay food and drink out on the altar, too.

Start by stating what the project is – what it's for, what its aims and objectives are and what you hope it will achieve. If there are others present, encourage them to each say a few words about their own hopes and expectations for the project. Next, affirm your commitment to the success of the project, and say what your role in it will be (along with, of course, anyone else who is there).

Write affirmations to put in amongst the good luck charms – something like, 'This project is a great success', 'This project is exhilarating to work on'. Include more specific ones, too, about what you intend to achieve.

Eat, drink and celebrate this new beginning.

Protect Yourself

Unless you're very lucky in your choice of environment, you're bound to meet unpleasant people and difficult situations in your everyday life. Unfortunately, negativity is even easier to pick up than the flu. Don't let it get to you and infect you. Protect yourself with these simple techniques that help you to shield your aura and stave off unwanted negative attacks.

Bubble of light

Build a bubble of light around yourself before going into a difficult situation and sense any negativity just bounce back off it.

YOU WILL NEED:

Just yourself

Breathe quietly and visualise a warm rainbow of light deep inside your heart. As you breathe gently and evenly, picture the light expanding until it surrounds you entirely in an all-enveloping rainbow bubble. Let the bubble solidify into a tough, durable skin and feel secure and at ease, knowing anything negative will just bounce right off its glimmering rainbow surface. Picture the difficult situation you are going into and see the negativity clearly bouncing right off that bouncy rainbow bubble. Imagine negativity being hurled at you from every quarter while you sit happily in your bubble watching it all just bounce off again.

Guardian amulet

Make a protective talisman to guard you from harm. Remember, though, it will only protect your aura. If you think you are in danger, take common sense, practical steps to protect yourself.

YOU WILL NEED:

A piece of jewellery – neck chain, pendant, bracelet, etc. Something with meaningful symbolism such as a cross or a pentagram works well

White candle and something to engrave it with

Inscribe the candle with the rune of protection, Elhaz ᛉ. Light the candle and sit calmly and peacefully holding your chosen piece of jewellery. Visualise a bright white light deep inside your heart. Breathe deeply and quietly and picture the light expanding until it envelops you completely within a radiant bubble. Let the bubble solidify into a dazzling ball of light with a mirror surface. Feel secure and safe inside this ball of light, knowing anything negative will just be reflected right back to its source. Visualise some situations you might find yourself in and see the negativity clearly reflecting back off the protective ball of light surrounding you, leaving you untouched and unharmed.

Hold your piece of jewellery up to the candle flame. Compress that dazzling ball of light and pour it all into the jewellery. Force it all in until the piece vibrates with light and protective power. Put it on. When you need protection, touch your talisman and you will immediately sense yourself surrounded by that dazzling ball of light reflecting back all the negativity.

Guardian spirits

Sometimes you need something more active than a bubble of light, however resilient that may be. Use this ritual with care, though. It will certainly keep negativity at bay when you are feeling at your most vulnerable, but it can also be a bit isolating, cutting you off from positivity as well.

YOU WILL NEED:

An animal talisman – a small figure or charm representing a powerful animal: wolf's tooth, bear claw, or representation of dog, lion, etc

White candle and something to engrave it with

Inscribe the candle with Elhaz ᚣ , the rune of protection. Light it and sit holding your animal talisman. Visualise the light deep inside your heart and let it expand until it envelops you completely in a dazzling globe of light. Imagine two guardian animals stand with you inside the light – mastiffs, lions, grizzly bears, whatever you have chosen. Feel these big, powerful creatures beside you, walking with you, and know you are secure and safe.

Visualise some situations where you feel insecure and replay them with your powerful guardians beside you. Remember, you control them completely.

Hold your totem animal up to the candle flame. Push all the light that surrounds you into that talisman. Imagine it glowing and vibrating with protective power. Carry it with you. Whenever you touch the talisman, you will sense your guardian animals beside you, surrounded with light.

Charms and Talismans

Charms and talismans have a wider use than just protection. Draw on them in all sorts of way to enhance your life.

Serenity charm

A talisman to keep you calm and serene.

YOU WILL NEED:

A piece of silver jewellery

A white candle

A full moon

Soft, sweet music

Light the candle. Sit holding your piece of jewellery in sight of the full moon and listen to the music. Watch the moon sailing through the sky and let your thoughts become still and tranquil. Inhale that cool silver light, breathing it deeply into your soul. Visualise the moonlight beginning to fill your entire body with radiance. Let it fill you and grow beyond you, surrounding you with a pearly glow. You and the moon are one, sailing far above it all.

Let your thoughts drift back to a time, real or imagined, when you felt completely peaceful and at ease. Hold your talisman up to the moon and visualise pouring all the peace and serenity within you and surrounding you at this moment into that piece of silver jewellery. See it glowing with moon-magic.

Keep the talisman by you and hold it in your hand whenever you want to re-experience that tranquillity. Re-charge your charm by repeating the ritual at every full moon.

Energy charm

A talisman to fire you up.

YOU WILL NEED:

A piece of gold or gold-coloured jewellery

A red candle

Energetic music

Light the candle and sit holding your piece of jewellery. Listen to the music and let it begin to dance in your blood. Feel your feet wanting to tap to the beat. Breathe in the hot red energy from the candle flame. Breathe it deep into your soul. Visualise the light and the music filling your entire body with sparkling energy. Let it fill you and expand beyond you, surrounding you with shooting stars of vivacity. Get up and dance if you want. Imagine fireworks surrounding you.

Cast your thoughts back to a time when you felt completely alive and energised. Hold your talisman up to the candle flame and visualise pouring all the energy within and around you into the charm. Imagine pushing even more energy in, forcing it in until it fizzes and sparkles with life.

Keep the talisman by you and hold it in your hand whenever you need a shot of energy. Re-charge your charm frequently for maximum impact.

Freedom charm

Recapture the feeling you had on holiday that anything could happen.

YOU WILL NEED:

Something brought back from your holiday – a seashell, for example

A white candle, a blue candle and a green candle

Music or sounds (waves on the shore, perhaps) that remind you of your holiday

Light the candles. Hold your holiday talisman in your hand and listen to the music or sounds you have chosen. Let the blue, green and white light of the candles weave itself into the sound and inhale it deeply, drawing it into your soul. Let your thoughts recapture that holiday sense of newness and freshness, the feeling you are free to do exactly as you wish and all possibilities are open to you. Free of stress, free of expectations, free of commitments. Free of all the shoulds, oughts and musts of everyday life. Breathe it all in, breathing it deeply into your heart. Visualise it filling your entire body, lifting your heart, clearing your mind and energising your body. Hold your talisman up to the candle flames and visualise pouring all those feelings into it. Feel it vibrate with stored power.

Keep your talisman with you and hold it in your hand to recapture that spirit of freedom whenever everyday things threaten to get on top of you. Re-charge your charm often to keep up the power.

Heart's delight charm

This charm will keep your soul intact in difficult circumstances.

YOU WILL NEED:

A pressed flower

A silver candle

For the best effect, go somewhere you love and feel peaceful in – a garden, a park, out into the countryside – and pick one flower to press specifically for this charm. (Press between two sheets of blotting paper under a heavy book or something similar and leave for a few days.)

Light the candle and sit with your pressed flower. Visualise the silvery light from the candle spinning itself into a silver mist around you. Breathe in the radiance, pulling it deeply into you. Imagine walking through the mist and emerging into a beautiful, sun-lit garden. See the flowers and the butterflies; hear the birds and the gentle splash of a distant fountain; feel the soft grass under your feet and the warm breeze on your skin. Know you are completely safe and at peace in this garden. You spot a particular flower haloed with a soft, silver light. Pick this flower and keep it with you as you bring your thoughts back to the here and now.

Look at the pressed flower you hold in your hand and visualise it merging with that radiant flower from the garden. Keep the flower with you, in a locket, for example, or taped into your diary or address book. Look at it to experience a moment's peace back in that enchanted garden. Re-charge your charm whenever you feel it's necessary.

Another way of charging a charm with enchantment is to literally bathe in its influence. Run a hot bath. Surround it with candlelight and try one of the following charm-laden rituals.

Beauty charm

Bathe yourself in the beauty of the rose to incorporate it into your aura.

YOU WILL NEED:

A handful of rose petals

Rose essential oil

One fresh rose

Scatter the rose petals on the water and add a couple of drops of rose oil. Get into the bath, hold the rose in your hands and relax. Let the golden light of the candles mingle with the scent of the rose oil and the petals and breathe it in, drawing it deeply into yourself. Feel the light filling you, visualise every cell of your body filling with scented brilliance. Picture the light surrounding you so you glow with a rose-gold radiance.

Gaze at the rose in your hand and draw the beauty into yourself along with the light and the scent. Imagine the loveliness of it flowing into your aura, soaking through your skin and right into your heart and soul. Feel your entire body vibrating and glowing with its luminous beauty.

After your bath, either take a couple of petals from the rose, press them and keep them, or dry the entire rose. The petals or dried flower will be your talisman. Keep it with you in a locket, bag or pouch, or tape the petals into a book or diary. Look at them to re-awaken the beauty of the rose in your aura.

Repeat as and when you like with fresh roses.

Strength charm

A heart of oak can be yours if you strengthen your aura with this charm.

YOU WILL NEED:

A handful of oak leaves

Oak moss essential oil (or sandalwood if you can't find any)

An acorn

Scatter the oak leaves into your bath and add a couple of drops of the essential oil. Relax in the bath, holding the acorn in your hand. Let the pungent scent of the oil merge with the light of the candles. Imagine the light filtering through the dense leaves of a forest oak tree, mysteriously green and gold. Breathe it in, pulling it right into your heart. Sense the light surrounding you and filling your body with that emerald radiance. Visualise yourself becoming that tree; feel the massive size and power and the vast age and strength of it. Feel your roots plunging deep into the earth, great branches spreading up into the sky. Feel the sun pouring strength and life into you. Draw the strength of the earth up through your roots. Imagine it flowing into you, drawing it right into your heart and soul. Feel your entire body vibrating and glowing with power and strength.

Look at the acorn in your hand, pour all the strength of the oak into it along with all the light and scent. After your bath, keep the acorn with you as a talisman. Look at it to re-awaken the power of the oak within you. Repeat the ritual often.

Grace charm

The graceful willow provides the inspiration for this charm.

YOU WILL NEED:

A handful of willow leaves

Lavender essential oil

A length of thin, supple willow twig about 45cm (18in.) long

Add a couple of drops of oil to the bath and scatter the willow leaves on the surface. Hold the willow wand in your hands as you relax in the water. Let the pale gold light of the candles blend with the scent of the oil and breathe it in. Draw it deep into your body and feel yourself becoming lighter and more radiant as the shimmering glow fills you.

Picture the shimmering reflection of a willow tree dancing on the surface of the water. Feel the sway of it in your own body. Feel the light filling you, and let your body ripple with the water and the willow. Feel the grace of the swaying branches gently entering your own limbs right down to your finger- and toe-tips. Visualise every cell of your body filling with grace. Picture that pale gold light surrounding you with an aura of grace.

Gaze at the willow wand in your hand and visualise all the

grace of the tree flowing into it along with the light and scent. Tie it into a loose knot or ring so you can keep it with you more easily. Look at it to re-awaken the grace of the willow within you. Repeat the ritual whenever you feel it to be necessary.

Bundle of charm

Try this Medicine Bundle talisman from the Native American tradition to keep luck, good feelings and personal power at hand.

YOU WILL NEED:

Natural objects that have some meaning or symbolism for you – crystals, stones, seeds, feathers, shells, etc. You could use a shell from a holiday beach, a pebble from a favourite walk, a fossil, a feather that reminds you to feel light-hearted, one of your baby teeth, a sprig of lavender from your garden ...

A piece of cloth that reflects your character – some people are silk, others suede, hessian or lace, etc. If you like, make the fabric into a small bag or pouch, or just use it as a wrapping

A cord or ribbon

A candle and something to engrave it with

Incense

A bowl of water

A stone

Inscribe the rune of transformation, Eoh ↲, onto the candle and light it. Put the stone, water and incense with it. Gather your objects together and spend some time looking at them and holding them and sensing their significance for you. Wrap them in the cloth and tie the cord securely around it.

Infuse the bundle with the power of the four elements. Hold the bundle up to the candle flame and visualise all the energy of fire being drawn into it, along with the power of transformation. Draw the energy into your own soul at the same time.

Pass the bundle through the incense smoke and picture the clarity of air entering it. Breathe in the incense and draw that feeling into your body and your mind at the same time. Sense anything connected with air in your bundle – feathers, for example – becoming energised and filled with power.

Touch the bundle to the stone and imagine all the power of the earth passing into it. Pull the strength into yourself also. Feel anything in your bundle connected with the earth responding.

Finally, sprinkle the bundle with a few drops of the water and feel the spirit of the ocean enter it. Sense any items such as shells and pebbles in your bundle becoming infused with the power of the tides. Draw some of that power into yourself, too.

Hold the medicine bundle in your hands and visualise the power of the elements working within you. Carry it with you to remind you of your connection to them.

Accentuate the Positive

As well as using rituals to banish negativity from yourself and protect you against other people's negativity, you can also use them to open yourself up to positive energy. Try these rituals to light up your life.

Rainbow of light

Open yourself up to the influence of colour in your life, both literally and metaphorically, with this ritual.

YOU WILL NEED:

A candle for each colour of the rainbow:

RED *for energy, vitality and love*

ORANGE *for friendship, hospitality and warmth*

YELLOW *for courage, communication and joy*

GREEN *for growth and prosperity*

LIGHT BLUE *for healing and peace*

DARK BLUE *for vision and clarity*

VIOLET *for spirituality and wisdom*

SILVER *for dreams*

GOLD *for blessings*

Arrange the candles in a circle if you can make one big enough for you to sit in safely. Otherwise, arrange the candles in front of you so you can see each one. Light the candles and sit before them or in the middle of them. Visualise the candle flames gradually weaving themselves into a shimmering rainbow mist around you.

Imagine you are walking through a rainbow. See each colour as you feel yourself step into it. Feel it; inhale it, let it flow into you, filling you with that colour. Red first, warm and empowering, then orange, yellow, green, all the way through to gentle, spiritual violet. Next, find yourself bathed in a dreamy, silver light that lifts away all your negativity. Finally, a gold light envelops you, pouring radiance into you. Visualise it filling your life with love, warmth, joy, abundance, peace, security and hope. Breathe in the light and sense it flowing deeply into every part of you, filling you with the same.

Step out of the rainbow and return to the everyday world. Sit with the candles as long as you want.

Web of creation

Use this ritual to tune yourself to the positive vibrations of the world around you.

YOU WILL NEED:

A candle

This is a good ritual to do outside, if you possibly can, in the quietness of dark or dusk. Light the candle. Sit and take a few moments to simply notice the scents and sounds and sensations around you. Let your senses expand until those faint sounds and scents you would normally never notice become apparent to you.

Close your eyes and visualise yourself at the centre of a web of connected threads. Through each thread you feel faint vibrations and sense the distant world. Let your senses flow out along each thread. Everything is connected to you and you are connected to everything. Feel yourself held in the web of creation.

Bring your senses back to your immediate environment. Sit for a while simply enjoying the quietness of a candlelit world.

Everyday magic

Make the most of every positive experience you come across.

YOU WILL NEED:

Just yourself

When you encounter a wonderful sunset, your first glimpse of the ocean, a wood full of bluebells, or anything else special and beautiful, feed your soul with it. Breathe it in and embrace it. Visualise opening your heart and inhaling it deeply into yourself, pulling it right into your heart and soul. Sense the glow of the good feeling of it flow into some deep, central part of you. It only takes a moment, but it will stay with you for ever.

Chapter Seven

Charmed Relationships

Friendly souls

Family, friends, colleagues, lovers – relationships play an important part in life. This chapter looks at how rituals enhance communication with others. It explores ways and means of clearing negative feelings and misunderstandings, and bringing balance, pleasure and fulfilment to the ups and downs of everyday interactions.

Whether you want to get closer to someone or build healthy boundaries, a little enchantment goes a long way towards helping you achieve the relationships you want. How do you find your place in a group? How can you celebrate a new love? How can you psych yourself up to deal with someone who's getting too close, fan the flames of a new relationship or ginger up an established one? Read on.

Resolving Conflict

Even the sunniest relationships have their off days. There will always be periods when you go through conflict and dispute but rituals can help you resolve things in your own mind so you quickly heal the breach and smooth things over.

Burying the hatchet

This ritual should help release your mind from past grudges with friends or colleagues, leaving you free to move on with a lighter heart.

YOU WILL NEED:

A stone

A piece of paper and a pen

A white candle

A potted sage plant

A length of white ribbon

A patch of earth, large plant pot or a window box

Light the candle and take a moment to focus on your intention – to bury this grudge firmly and finally. By the light of the candle, write your grudge down as fully as you wish on the paper. As you write, visualise all the rancour flowing out and away from you and into the paper. See the paper become dark, heavy and sodden with it as you become lighter and freer.

Draw a firm, heavy line under your writing saying, 'This is the finish of it, this is the end.' Sit quietly in the candlelight for a moment, sensing the flame gently burning away any lingering negativity. Wrap the paper tightly around the stone, and bind them both with the ribbon.

Still in a positive state of mind, bury your grudge deep in the earth. (Snuff the candle if you have to go outside, rather than leave it unattended.) Visualise the healing earth dissolving the poison out of it, neutralising it. Plant the sage on top – sage is a healing and purifying plant.

Water the sage and look after it to remind you of your happy release. If you want to be really healing, prepare a reconciliatory meal, flavour it with the sage, and invite the person you held the grudge against to enjoy it with you.

Healing the rift

Here's another ritual to help heal a rift between you and someone else.

YOU WILL NEED:

A photograph of you

A photograph of the other person – if you haven't got one, find something that symbolises them to you

A jar of honey and a spoon

A length of white ribbon

Do this by candlelight or daylight, whichever you prefer. Hold the photo or symbol in your hand and focus on it. Tell this person everything you want to say to them. Really get it off your chest, but try to remember you are healing the breach between you, not working up an even stronger grudge.

When you have said everything you need to say, collect your thoughts and take a spoonful of honey. Enjoy the sweetness on your tongue and recall something you like and/or admire about this person. Look at their picture or symbol, take another spoonful of honey and think of another thing you like about them. Keep going until you genuinely can't think of anything else.

Put the photos together, face to face, and wrap the white ribbon around them (or wrap your photo and their symbol together). Put the ribbon bundle somewhere safe. If it's possible and reasonable, go to see the other person, call them or write to them, and sort things out between you as soon as possible.

Deepening Connections

Try these rituals when you want to get closer to friends or relatives and strengthen the bonds between you.

New friend

Welcome a new friend or family member into your life with this ritual.

YOU WILL NEED:

> *A large orange candle – a pillar candle or a wide flat one or an especially ornate one would be nice*
>
> *About a dozen small candles – tea lights or night lights, for example*
>
> *A handful of grain – rice, lentils or barley would do*
>
> *A handful of gravel or small stones*

Put the orange candle in the centre and light it. Keep one of the small candles to one side to represent your new friend and put the rest in a circle around the orange one. Surround the candles with a ring of grain. Surround the ring of grain with an outer ring of gravel. Light the candles.

Look at the ring of gravel and recall how daunting and impenetrable a close-knit group can look from the outside. Look at the ring of grain and spend a little time remembering how fruitful belonging to this group or family has been for you – what you've gained and what you've contributed. Look at the circle of candles and let your thoughts linger over the people currently in the group – remember times you've enjoyed together, things you've done and the experiences you've had.

Put the remaining candle with the others. If you have to rearrange them slightly to get the new one in, think about the adjustments you might have to make to include this new member. As you light the candle, welcome this new person into your circle. Think about them and what you like about them. Think about what you're looking forward to about having them in the group, and what pleasures they'll bring and gifts they'll contribute. Let the candles burn down naturally.

Thinking of you

Give the gift of your good wishes to a friend.

YOU WILL NEED:

Two orange candles

An attractive plant pot

Potting compost

Pen and paper

A greetings card

A potted plant

Light the candles and, by their light, reflect on your friendship with the other person. See their face in one of the candle flames and tell them about the pleasure your relationship brings you.

Tear the paper into small slips and, on each one, write a wish for your friend's future. 'May you always be happy', might be one, 'May you find true love' or 'May the sun shine on you' might be others, or you might have specific things you want to wish them based on your knowledge of their circumstances. Pick one of the wishes and write it into the greetings card.

Pour a little potting compost into the pot and bury your wish-covered papers in it. Plant the flower on top and present to your friend along with the card.

A few kind words

This makes an excellent present for someone who has a special birthday, anniversary, retirement or other special occasion coming up. It takes a bit of organising, but the results for the recipient of this gift are well worth the effort. It really helps to deepen connections all round.

YOU WILL NEED:

An attractively bound book or album

Friends, family and/or colleagues of the recipient

Simply ask people to write down a memory or anecdote about the birthday boy or girl (or colleague, or relative, or whatever the relationship is) to go into the album. Allow everyone enough time (a couple of weeks, say) to come up with something, but make it clear there's a deadline. One of the nice things about this is you can include people who live a long way away. Paste the reminiscences into the book and give it to the recipient – preferably at a party with most or all of the contributors present.

United we stand

When two or more of you want to establish your commitment to each other or to a joint venture, try this ritual loosely based on a traditional Gypsy ceremony for sealing an agreement.

YOU WILL NEED:

Red candles – one for each person

One glass

Red wine or some red juice if you want something non-alcoholic

Patch of earth, pot or window box

Potted plant with red flowers

Light a candle each. This symbolises the energy and commitment you each bring to the venture or relationship. Pour the wine or juice into one glass. This symbolises the shared life-blood of the people involved.

With each person drinking from the same glass, make a toast to each other and to the venture or the relationship. Smash the glass so this commitment can never be broken. Bury the small pieces of glass deep in the earth (where nobody can cut themselves on them) and plant the red flowers on top. Take care of the plant – as it thrives, so the venture or relationship will thrive.

Light of love

Feel closer to friends, family or your community with this ritual practised at regular intervals. Wishing people well nearly always makes you feel fonder of them.

YOU WILL NEED:

White candle

Pen and paper

Light the candle. Think about the individual or community you would like to send your love and support to. Write their name (or the name of the group) on the paper and put it under the candle.

Picture these people in your mind's eye and visualise the candlelight spiralling upwards and outwards, forming itself into a cone of energy enveloping them all. Imagine it swirling round the people, surrounding them with love and light. Visualise them becoming filled with radiance and joy. Picture the cone of light energising them with health and happiness, driving out any negativity or darkness. Add your own good wishes to the light.

Carry out this ritual alone or in a group. In a group, take turns to add names to the paper, if you wish, and you might like to link hands before you start the visualisation. You can use the paper with the names on again, or start from scratch another time.

Your Place in the Group

Sometimes, finding your feet in a new group or organisation is difficult. When you change to a new job, move to a new neighbourhood or just find yourself in a new gang of friends, finding out where you belong, how you relate to the other people in it, even feeling you belong can sometimes be a challenge. Try this ritual to help your unconscious mind get to work on the problem.

Map of me

YOU WILL NEED:

Large sheet of paper or card

Photograph of you looking happy and relaxed

Photos or symbols of the other people involved – if you have nothing else, just write their names on slips of paper

Glue

Two orange candles and something to engrave them with – toothpick, needle, etc

Inscribe the candles with the rune Ehwaz M , which symbolises loyalty and support. Light them and lay out all your pictures, symbols, names and whatever else you have on the sheet of paper. Move them around until you feel you have achieved a representation of the group – is everybody equal or are some people at the top and others lower down a hierarchy? Are there some people in the middle with others more on the outside? Are there groups within the group? Take your time and use all your intuition to arrive at an arrangement.

If you haven't already included yourself, where do you fit in? Are you happy with where you are or would you like to fill a different position? Keep shifting things around until you feel comfortable with it. When you're happy, glue everything in position and put the resulting picture where you will see it often. If, after a few days, you decide you're not happy with where you've put yourself in the picture, you can always change it or make another one.

Changing the map

Sometimes, you know exactly where and how you fit in, but you want to change it! Try this ritual to help you make your move.

YOU WILL NEED:

Large sheet of paper or card

Photograph of you looking happy

Photos or symbols of the other people involved, or just write their names on pieces of paper

Glue

Two orange candles and something to engrave them with

This is essentially the same as the ritual above; use the pictures, photographs and symbols to create a picture of the group in the same way. This time, though, include yourself in the position you feel you currently occupy but don't glue anything down yet.

Take a moment to reflect on what you see. How do you feel about it? Seeing everything spread out before you like this, are there obvious changes you could make? Put yourself in the position you want to occupy. Keep shifting the patterns around until you achieve something you feel comfortable with. Glue everything in position and put the picture where you will see it regularly.

Love and Romance

Here's a collection of rituals to help you get closer to the one you love, whether that's a new love or a long established one.

Ribbons of love

Is there someone you want to entwine your life with? Make your commitment clear to yourself with this ritual. Remember, though, it's not magic – they won't automatically feel the same way about you. But if you think they might be open to persuasion, go ahead and give it a whirl.

YOU WILL NEED:

Three lengths of ribbon, each about a metre long, in three of your favourite colours

Pink candle plus something to engrave it with

Inscribe the rune of destiny, Mann ᛗ , on the candle and light it. Pick one of the ribbons to symbolise yourself. Hold it in your hand and think about why you want to interweave your life with this other person's. Pick another ribbon to symbolise the other person. Hold it in your hand and reflect on what it is about them that attracts you in this way. Take the third ribbon, which represents love. Hold it in your hand and consider relationships you have had in the past, how you feel about relationships in general, and what you think about this one in particular.

Knot the three ribbons together at the top and braid them together into one single plait. Visualise blending your two lives together with love as you do so. Knot the ends securely. Tie the braid around your wrist and wear it for the next week. Afterwards, keep it somewhere where you will see it frequently, or carry it with you in a bag or pocket.

If the relationship develops as you intend, put the braid under your shared pillow or mattress, or even tie it to the bed head. If things don't work out as you hoped, release yourself from your commitment by unravelling the braid and burning it.

Getting to know you

Some people like to rush into passion, others like to get to know each other better first. Whether you are in a new relationship or an old established one, try this ritual as a prelude to the main event. It will deepen the connection between you and give your mutual sensuality the chance to unfold.

YOU WILL NEED:

Pink and red candles

Towels

Massage oil

Soothing music

Lots of time and privacy

Light the candles and put the music on. Undress and sit facing each other. Taking it in turns, explore your partner's face and neck with your fingers. Move on to the back and arms. Continue to discover each other in this way, gradually introducing some feedback so you find out how each of you likes to be touched and where, but staying off the erogenous zones for the time being.

Spread the towels out on the floor or bed and take it in turns to give each other a full body massage. Start on the back and use gentle, sweeping movements over the skin. Don't worry about not being an expert masseur or masseuse, the point is physical contact and intimacy rather than physiotherapy.

After you've both had a massage, do what feels right for you. If you both want to take things further, then go with it. If not, finish the session with some light food and relaxed conversation. At this stage, you should feel very comfortable in each other's company.

A loving cup

What's wrong with a good old-fashioned love potion? Try this ritual to kindle the fires and strengthen the bonds between you.

YOU WILL NEED:

Red and pink candles

Soft music

A handful of fresh basil leaves

A light, white wine, or a non-alcoholic alternative such as spring water or grape juice

Easy-to-eat finger food

Basil is the herb of love in Italy, but its powers will work just as well in any other part of the world. Pour the wine over the basil leaves, saving a few fresh leaves to garnish, and leave in the fridge for an hour or so for the flavour to develop. Strain into a jug and decorate with the leaves.

Light the candles and put the music on. Enjoy the food and the wine. Use this as an opportunity to toast each other's finer points. Don't forget to snuff the candles before you leave the room.

When two become one

When things *do* work out between you, you might want a ceremony to celebrate your new, shared relationship with each other. See if the following one appeals.

YOU WILL NEED:

Two white candles

One big pillar candle

A wineglass

White wine or fruit juice

Pen and paper

Plant pot

Potted plant with white flowers

It's nice to have an altar as well for this ritual. Put photos of the two of you and souvenirs of your relationship on it, together with lots of flowers and greenery. Put the big pillar candle in the centre and the rest of the things around it. Write your names on a piece of paper and put this on the altar, too.

Light a white candle each. As you do so, tell your partner what you love about them, what you have enjoyed about the relationship up to now and what you hope for in the future. When you have both done this, light the central pillar candle from your own two, leaving all three to burn on the altar as a symbol of both your individual and newly combined lives.

Pour the wine or juice into the glass and make a toast to each other and to the future. After you have both drunk from it, smash the glass and bury it in the pot along with the slip of paper with your names on. Plant the white flowers on top and tend them very carefully. Seal your commitment with a kiss. A celebratory feast is a good idea, too.

New Baby

The following ritual needn't just apply to a newly-born baby; a stepchild coming into a new family of aunts, uncles and grand-parents, or an adopted child, all will benefit greatly from being formally welcomed into the family.

Fairy god-relatives

YOU WILL NEED:

A selection of beads

Leather thong or beading thread

Attractively bound book or album and a pen

Friends and relatives who will be in the child's life

An altar is a nice addition to this ritual, and a feast for afterwards. Dress the altar with lots of flowers, good luck symbols, any cards, congratulations or gifts, your hopes for the child's future, photos of the child, protective spirits and deities, soft toys, and such like.

Have all the beads ready in a bowl – one for each participant and a couple more for luck. Have the thread or thong ready with a firm knot at one end. It's a good idea to tell participants what you intend to do beforehand so they have time to think about it.

As formally or informally as you wish, get the participants into a group with the baby or child. Make a short speech 'introducing' the child into the group, in particular naming the child and stating their relationship to those present. Have each participant in turn choose a bead and hand it to the child along with a traditional 'fairy-godmother' blessing – 'May you have confidence and self-assurance', for example, or 'May you have a warm and loving heart', or 'May you have foresight and vision.' It's nice when people choose the qualities that have helped them in their own lives.

As each wish is made and each bead handed over, slip the beads onto the thong. (Save a lot of embarrassment by ensuring each bead has a big enough hole before the ceremony.) Either write down the name of the participant, their wish and their bead colour in the album as you go, or have everyone write it in their own handwriting at the end. Knot the other end of the thong to keep the beads safe and tie it securely round the child's wrist while everyone enjoys the feast. Later, thread the beads more securely, perhaps with a catch or fastener, so the child will have a permanent reminder of the occasion they can wear when older.

Cutting the Ties

While it's generally a good thing to have strong and loving connections to people, sometimes they become too much of a good thing and threaten to develop into a much less healthy sort of relationship. The following rituals can help you free yourself from a dependent or destructive relationship or get it onto a much better footing.

Disenchantment

Sometimes you feel more connected to someone than is good for either you or them. Increase your sense of personal space with the following ritual and set some healthy boundaries between you.

YOU WILL NEED:

A dark-coloured candle in a very stable holder and something to inscribe it with

Some building bricks, Lego bricks, or something similar

A bag or pouch

Inscribe the candle with the name of the person you need to be distanced from and underneath put the rune Isa **|** which symbolises an icicle and signifies a standstill. Light the candle and visualise the person's face in the candle flame. Explain to them firmly and clearly that you need some distance from them. Tell them how the relationship between you is going to be in the future – respectful but distant. Go through the history of your relationship and tell them what's wrong and why. As you do so, gradually push the candle with their name on it further and further away from you.

When it is as far away as it will go, build the bricks into a wall between you and the candle. Visualise a healthy detachment growing up between you both, a barrier neither of you feels inclined to bridge. See yourself behaving calmly and coolly with this person the next time you meet – polite but reserved. Say goodbye and snuff the candle.

Put a couple of the bricks in the bag or pouch and keep them with you the next time you have to see this person. If possible, casually put the bag on the table or desk between you to remind you of that barrier and your resolve to be detached.

Cut the ties

Sometimes even creating a breathing space is not enough and you need to deliberately cut the ties between you. When you feel that to be true, try this ritual for severing emotional and psychological connections.

YOU WILL NEED:

Paper and pen

Length of red ribbon

Scissors

Candles

Patch of earth, plant pot or window box

Stream, river or the sea

Sit quietly by candlelight holding the ribbon in your hands. Think about the person you feel tied to. Write their name on a slip of paper. Think about the relationship between you and visualise the other person sitting opposite you. Either in your mind or out loud, tell them why you need to break the tie with them. Explain to them it's time to release you both from the bondage of this relationship. Think about what you want for the future. You may still want a relationship with them, just not the sort you had in the past.

Picture an actual cord stretching between you and this person tying you firmly together. In your imagination, take a pair of scissors and cut the cord, releasing you both. If you need a more energetic image – and some people do – visualise taking an axe and using that. Feel the effort in your shoulders and arms as you swing, and the release as the blade bites through the cord. Sense the person drifting away from you, as if pulled by a relentless tide.

Take the scissors and cut the real ribbon in half. Wrap one piece around the piece of paper with their name on it and bury it in the earth. Keep the other piece with you and the next time you are passing running water, throw it in. (Or, of course, you could make a special journey to a river or stream, or the seaside to do it.)

Variation

If it's a relationship where you wish to keep the closeness, but without the previous feeling of a stranglehold – parent/adult child relationships can sometimes be like this – cut the ribbon as above and keep both halves, but in separate places at opposite ends of your home.

Heart of the matter

Sometimes it's your own feelings that need to be kept under lock and key if you are not to lose far more than you would ever gain. Outside temptations happen even in the strongest relationship. When you're tempted by forbidden fruit, try this ritual to cool your ardour.

YOU WILL NEED:

Three white candles

Drawing of a heart on a sheet of paper

Pen and paper

Small padlock

Freezerproof container

Water

Freezer

Put the three candles in a row and light the two outside ones. These represent you and any third person involved, or potentially involved, in the situation. The candle in the centre represents your would-be lover. Light this candle too, and by its flame think deeply about how you have come to this situation. Use the paper and pen to jot down any thoughts and ideas as they occur to you. Think about the things that might be missing from your life and consider how you will meet those needs by better means – who might you want to talk to, what might you want to do?

Visualise your would-be lover's face in the candle flame. Tell them clearly why this can go no further – why it's a bad idea and what you have to lose – and say goodbye. Snuff the flame with your thumb and finger (not your breath or you'll symbolically breathe new life into the relationship) and push the candle away from you.

Write your own name in the middle of the drawing of the heart. Roll it up and snap the padlock closed around it. Put them in the freezerproof container and pour the water over. Put your padlocked heart into the freezer and keep it there until you are sure the fires have cooled.

Letting Go

For one reason or another, it's the fate of some relationships to end. When this happens, ritual can bring a sense of proper closure and release.

River of life

When the life span of a friendship comes to its natural end, give thanks for what has been and move on.

YOU WILL NEED:

A photo or some other symbol of your friend

Pen and paper

Silver ribbon

A river, stream or other running water

If possible, do this ritual in a quiet spot near running water. If not, do the first part at home and go to a river or stream to complete it. Sit quietly and contemplate the photo or symbol of your friend. Visualise their face and tell them what you have enjoyed about your friendship, what has been of value, and what you hope to take from it into the future. Say goodbye to them.

Write down a short 'epitaph' on the paper – something like, 'Tina, you were my best friend at school. We grew up together and you were always there for me when I needed your help. You ... etc, etc ... But now we've grown up and grown apart as our lives have gone in different directions. I will always value our friendship and you will always be a part of me because you were there when I was growing up and becoming me, just as I will always be a part of you for the same reason ...' Close with a goodbye and your best wishes for their future.

Roll the photo or symbol up with the paper and tie with the silver ribbon. Throw it into the water and release it into the current. Let the flow take it where it will.

Letting the soul go

It can be hard to let go of someone who has died, even after you have grieved for them fully. Try this gentle ritual if you feel you still need to release the soul of someone close to you.

YOU WILL NEED:

Plenty of time

Candles to mark out a circle on the floor

Photograph of the person

Envelope

Make a circle with the candles. Light them and sit inside it with the photograph and envelope. Take time to remember and commemorate the person you have lost. Look at their photograph and visualise them there with you. Say all things you want to say to them, express all your thoughts.

Close your eyes and visualise the light from the candles gently spiralling upwards from the circle. Release the soul you have been clinging on to into it. Imagine it being tenderly borne upwards. Visualise its ascent into an even greater light.

When you are ready, open your eyes. Put the photograph in the envelope and put them both away somewhere safe and special. Snuff the candles.

Chapter Eight

Working Wonders

Soul survivors

This chapter looks at rituals that improve your working day and help smooth out the potholes in your career path. Most of us spend half our waking lives at work, if not longer, so any tips on making it more enjoyable can only be welcome.

Although useful as a guide for anyone interested in success, this isn't magic and doing the rituals will not, unfortunately, result in huge sums of money flowing miraculously into your bank account. Nor will they help if you expect success without effort. They will, however, help you attain your own highest potential and thereby attract your fair share of support, prospects and opportunities.

Wonder work

Some people seem to fall on their feet when it comes to employment. They love their job, have plenty of interesting work, are always being offered new opportunities, and appear to go from strength to strength with very little trouble. If this is not you, see if the following rituals help.

In the picture

When you feel less than enthusiastic about your job – apathetic, disconnected, uninvolved – this ritual could help you to feel more a part of what's going on and make it easier for you to take a central role at work.

YOU WILL NEED:

Large sheet of paper or card

Pictures that symbolise your job and your workplace in a positive way – cut them from brochures, magazines, publicity material, etc

Glue

A photograph of yourself (preferably one where you are smiling)

Two candles

Collect together all the pictures and put the photograph of yourself to one side. Light the candles to remind your unconscious you are doing something special. Paste the pictures onto the sheet of paper or card to make a pleasing collage. Take your time and enjoy 'playing'.

Spend a few minutes contemplating the picture you have made, concentrating on the positive impression it presents.

Paste the photograph of yourself right in the very centre. Put the finished collage where you will see it every day.

VARIATIONS

If you're feeling neglected or overlooked at work, make the collage as above then use a gold marker pen to draw a magnificent ornamental frame around your photograph. If you feel particularly playful, decorate your frame with things such as ribbons, flowers, beads or sequins.

If you feel something is missing from your working life, include lots of pictures that symbolise it in your collage.

If you feel disconnected from or disenchanted with specific aspects of your job, make up the collage as above and include pictures that represent whatever you're having difficulties with. Fix lengths of gold ribbon between your photograph and these pictures to symbolically reconnect you.

Career unblocker

When your career seems stagnant and you either lack the energy to move forward or feel unsure of your next step try this ritual to lift yourself out of the doldrums.

YOU WILL NEED:

A stairway

Something that represents career success

Objects that represent obstacles or stumbling blocks to your success – one for each step of the stairway

*Piece of gold ribbon long enough to reach from
the bottom of the stairs to the top*

Wastepaper bin

Bell

Please be very, very careful doing this ritual. Take your time, make sure the stairs are well lit and nobody else will need to use them while you are working.

Put the object representing success at the top of the stairs and arrange your 'obstacles' on the rest of the steps. Choose whatever makes sense to you. Maybe a clock if you feel time is your problem, a rag doll if you lack strength or a pile of papers if you get bogged down in paperwork. A picture of a closed mouth might represent your inability to speak out, or a pile of un-ironed clothes the domestic chores that sap your energy. Place the wastepaper bin at the bottom of the stairs.

Ring the bell to signal the start of the ritual. Pick the first object off the bottom step, think about what it represents for a moment, then put it in the bin. Move on to the next step and the next object and do the same. Slowly clear a path up the stairs, putting each obstacle in the bin at the bottom. (Yes, this does mean several trips up and down. Nobody said success was effortless.) When all your obstacles are in the bin lift it up and feel the weight of it. That's what was between you and your career goal.

Anchor one end of the golden ribbon under the bin. Climb the stairs – one last time – and tie the other end around the object symbolising success. Hold this object in your hands and feel the joy of having attained it after so much effort. With a gentle tug, free the end of the ribbon still trapped under the bin. Now success is truly yours.

213

Wrap the ribbon round the object and put it somewhere prominent. After a few days, unwind the ribbon and just leave the object where you'll see it. If you can take it to work with you, even better. Keep the ribbon and, when you need a career boost, cut a short length to tie around your wrist to remind yourself how you conquered those obstacles.

VARIATIONS

If it's your own thoughts and uncertainties that are getting in your way, write each 'yes, but …' and 'what if …' on a slip of paper and put these on each stair. Crumple each one up energetically before throwing in the bin.

If excuses are holding you back, treat them as above.

When you feel frustrated but can't identify your blocks, use bricks or stones to represent them. If you feel unfocused, try tangles of fluffy wool to symbolise your problem.

Career climber

Stairs are also very useful for this simple everyday ritual to boost your energy and motivation. Every time you walk up any stairs, take a deep breath and visualise climbing up above any problems towards ultimate success. Feel the sense of satisfaction and achievement when you reach the top. Coming down, visualise stepping down into a relaxed and firmly grounded state.

You can do a similar thing in lifts, of course. Going up, imagine lifting above any worries or troubles, rising into clear air and sunlight. Going down, imagine relaxing, floating gently down and coming to rest.

Busy bee

Every job goes through quiet patches but when every day starts dull, stays dull, and boring would be an improvement, something needs to change. Things just ticking over? Not enough to do? No excitement? Try this ritual to increase your energy and sensitise your unconscious mind to opportunities.

YOU WILL NEED:

Beeswax candle

Rosemary essential oil

Piece of green silk or cotton cloth

Light the beeswax candle. Sit quietly and visualise a herb garden full of sunlight and sweet-scented herbs, such as lavender, thyme and sage. Relax and feel the sun warm on your skin. Place a drop or two of the rosemary oil on the green cloth and breathe in the scent as you visualise. Imagine rubbing the leaves between your fingers and smelling the pungent scents. Listen to the hum of bees busy in the herb beds. Watch as they buzz around the flowers gathering pollen – purposeful, focused and happy.

Let your imagination drift to your workplace. As you look at the scene, see the place fill with the same swarm of bright bees. Hear their cheerful hum and smell the scent of herbs again. Breathe in the scent of the rosemary oil and feel your unconscious mind get to work. As you do so, see your workplace become a hive of industry. See yourself happy and busy, your colleagues cheerfully engaged. Hear the contented buzz of productivity.

When you feel the visualisation is complete, blow out the candle. Take the rosemary-scented cloth to work with you and enjoy the scent when you need energising.

Honey moon

When you're stuck in a job that isn't what you want – whether you're waiting for your ideal job to come up, waiting to qualify, preparing to start your own business, earning money to fund your real vocation, whatever – it can be hard finding the motivation and energy to keep going. This ritual sweetens the pill and helps you love what you're doing until you're doing what you love.

YOU WILL NEED:

Beeswax candle

Jar of honey and a spoon

Pen with gold ink

Paper

Red ribbon

Something that represents your workplace – a business card or company letterhead or logo would be suitable

Light the beeswax candle. Eat a spoonful of honey and begin thinking about the things you like about your job, its good points and advantages. Using the gold pen, write down every positive feature you can think of. Ask yourself:

- What do I like about my job?
- What do I like about where I work?
- What do I like about the people I work with?
- What are the pleasant moments in my day?
- What are the positive benefits of my job?
- Is there anything I can do that would improve the situation?
- What am I learning that will help me later?

As you consider each question take another spoonful of honey. When you've finished your list, fold up the paper with the object representing your workplace inside. Wrap round the outside of the honey jar and tie with the red ribbon. Every other day, unwrap your list and read it through while enjoying another spoonful of honey. If you find you can add to the list, so much the better.

Business express

While you're looking for your ideal job get your unconscious mind on your side with this simple but powerful ritual. You may want to do it over two nights – making up the collage one evening and doing the rest of the ritual on the next.

A collage like the one in In the picture above, with pictures and photographs that symbolise everything you want from your new position, and a photograph of yourself in the centre

A white candle

A blank business card (or piece of card the same size)

Gold pen

Light the candle and put your collage in front of you. Gaze at the picture you have made and let yourself enter into it. Imagine being in that environment. As you do so, see the things that will give you pleasure in your new job, hear pleasant sounds around you, and most of all experience the pleasure and satisfaction you will feel there.

Let the candle burn down as you thoroughly enjoy the taste of your perfect job. Keep bringing your attention back to the picture and experience that sense of certainty and success. Let the conviction grow inside you that this is the right thing for you.

Take the blank business card and write your name and ideal job title or occupation on it with the gold pen, for example, Jane Smith, Textile Designer; Karen Brown, Oceanographer; Tim Jones, Writer. Put the collage in a prominent position where you will see it every day. Put your new 'business card' in your purse or wallet, take it out and look at it often.

Take charge of your day

Wouldn't it be nice if you could start your day with purpose and vigour, replenish your energy throughout the day and thoroughly release all your stress at the end of it? Rituals provide a structure and rhythm to help you channel your energy so you get the most out of work and still have plenty left when you're ready to rest or play.

Begin the new day by focusing and connecting so you start off calm and in control. Try these empowering rituals when you want things to go your way.

Priorities

Try this ritual before work to connect you to the day ahead.

YOU WILL NEED:

Some incense

Sheet of paper

Pen with gold ink

Red ribbon

Light the incense. As you breathe in the scent, think about what you really want to get out of the day and what you want to have achieved by the end of it. Include practical tasks such as 'I want to get that report finished', and more personal goals such as 'I want to end the day feeling calm and relaxed'.

Write down the most important thing, then the next most important, and so on until you have a list of your priorities for the day. (Why the gold pen? Because your priorities are important, of course.) Fold the paper and roll it up tightly. Tie the red ribbon around it and pass it through the smoke of the incense – an ancient way of blessing things and sealing promises.

Carry the rolled list with you. Just knowing it's there is often enough to keep you on track but if you feel yourself slipping unroll it and remind yourself of your priorities. Tie it up again afterwards.

Your place in the sun

YOU WILL NEED:

Sunny window or garden

Glass of orange or grapefruit juice

Bell

Choose a sunny morning before work. Ring the bell above your head to dispel any lingering drowsiness and alert your unconscious mind. As the vibrations of the bell fade, become aware of the sun on your skin and the sparkle and glint of light. Take the glass of fruit juice and hold it up to the light. Recall how the sun warmed and ripened the fruit. Look at the glow of colour and imagine it becoming full of the energy of the sun.

Drink half the juice. Close your eyes and let the light flow into you. Imagine it filling you like a clear, golden liquid as you meditate on the power of the sun, a ball of unimaginable energy, the source of all life. Feel that strength and power become a part of you.

Finish the glass of juice and imagine you are drinking pure sunlight. Take a carton to work with you and pour a glassful to recapture your moment in the sun.

Take a break

Use lunchtime to refresh body and soul. Take a break to re-balance yourself or lift your spirits depending on what the morning has thrown at you and what the afternoon has in store. Perhaps you need to replenish your psychic and emotional energy, as well as satisfy physical hunger? Use the symbolism inherent in food to turn your lunchtime meal into a mood-enhancing ritual.

Soul food

Feeling spaced out? Can't concentrate? Lunch on a warming, grounding, baked potato to bring you back down to earth.

If, on the other hand, you feel too earth-bound and need to lighten up for the afternoon ahead, try lunching on 'living' foods – fresh juices or smoothies, sprouted beans or seeds.

When you need fiery energy to protect yourself or put your point across with passion and spirit, chilli should put you in a scorching mood. And don't forget to enjoy a spoonful of honey whenever you need to sweet-talk someone.

Walking back to happiness

If you can get out into the open air during your lunch break, use this ritual to harmonise body, mind and spirit and remind yourself of the bigger picture.

YOU WILL NEED:

A place to walk – park, gardens or some other green, open space

Packet of unsalted nuts (or raisins if you have a nut allergy)

Imagine you are stepping into another world and leaving the everyday one behind. Each nut or raisin represents a negative thought, worry or anxiety. As you walk, throw them away from you one at a time, naming the thought if you can and saying to yourself 'that gets rid of you'. Birds will soon come and eat the nuts (hence unsalted), so imagine all your negativity being transformed into birdie pleasure.

Pick up any small, pretty things you come across and give them meaning. A feather, for example, could symbolise lightness of heart; a daisy, freshness and innocence; an acorn could represent strength. You should find yourself in a very different frame of mind at the end of your walk than you were at the beginning.

Top of the world

Here's another outdoor lunchtime ritual to restore and rebalance your spirit.

YOU WILL NEED:

Just yourself and somewhere to sit

If you can, sit facing South – usually the direction of the sun – but don't worry too much about it. Sit quietly and let your breathing become slow and calm. Become aware of where you are. Feel the sun on your skin, the breeze lifting your hair, your feet firm on the ground. Imagine yourself as the balanced centre of a great compass.

Behind you is North, the place of wisdom. Sense the cool strength of mountains supporting you, the unstoppable power of glaciers at your back.

East is on your left, the direction of inspiration. Think of fresh winds and great sweeps of sky uplifting and exhilarating you, freeing your mind and your thoughts.

To the front of you is the fiery South, place of transformation and renewal. Feel the heat, and let the vibrant colour and passion of the South stir your excitement and enthusiasm, rekindling your energy.

To your right is the West, the direction of peace. Imagine a warm West wind blowing over the ocean at sunset, bringing healing and rest for you.

Spend as long as you need with each direction. Bring yourself back to the centre, then go back to work, refreshed.

The end of the day

End your working day by completing and releasing, ready to enjoy the evening ahead. However, many of us find it hard to switch off. Do you tend to spend the evening either still in work mode or flopped on the sofa in couch-potato mode? You clearly need a ritual, such as those below, to help you make the transition from work to play.

Completing

Definitively finish your working day with a simple closing ceremony.

YOU WILL NEED:

Pen and paper

First, let go of future worries by writing down everything you have to do tomorrow. When you have listed everything, draw a line firmly beneath it.

Tidy your desk or workspace and put away everything you can. Gather everything left on your desk into a neat pile and put your list of tasks face down on top. With the forefinger of your writing hand, mark it with Jera ♢ the rune of completion. Say to yourself, 'This is done, the day is done and now it is closed.' If you work with machines or computers turn them off and do the same.

Changing focus

Unharness your mind from your work and turn it in a different direction. Try the following ritual if you have difficulties detaching yourself.

YOU WILL NEED:

Something that symbolises work – a business card, or something you use at work

Something that symbolises the coming evening – maybe a picture of your family, or an item that reminds you it's party time

Piece of ribbon – red if you want a lively evening, blue if you prefer to be calm

If you can, light a candle. Otherwise, take a few deep breaths to relax and focus your mind. Take the symbol of work in your left hand and your symbol for the evening in your right. Hold both hands to your forehead for a few minutes while you think about your work life and your home life and the balance between them. Relax and rest your hands on the desk.

Open your left hand and look at your symbol of work. Think back over the day and choose two positive things that have happened. Give thanks for each of them, then, mentally, release them and let go. Either put your work symbol face down on the desk to signify it is finished or put it away in a drawer.

Open your right hand to show the symbol of your evening. Look at this symbol while thinking ahead of what you plan to enjoy. Choose two positive things you intend to happen then mentally release these, too, and let go. Wrap the ribbon around your symbol for the evening and take it home with you.

Regain your marbles

When you've had a run of bad days and it feels like everyone has got a piece of you except you, use this ritual at home to re-knit your ravelled soul. Allow plenty of time.

YOU WILL NEED:

> *A picture of the human body about A4-sized – a drawing, or largish photograph. Draw a red heart in the middle of the chest before you begin*
>
> *Scissors*
>
> *Seven candles*
>
> *Paper or card and paste*
>
> *Gold marker pen*

Arrange the seven candles in a semi-circle in front of you, leaving yourself room to work. Light the first one. Cut the picture into six pieces so you have:

- Feet and legs
- Lower body up to the waist
- Chest with heart
- Throat and mouth
- Rest of the head

- Hands and arms (this might be two pieces depending on the picture)

Shuffle the bits so they are thoroughly scattered and muddled. Reflect on your own scattered, muddled feelings and promise to restore yourself to harmony and completeness.

Find the piece with the feet and legs. Light another candle. Do your own legs feel strong, or are they weak and tired? Do you feel you stand on your own two feet? Can you make great strides forward or do you feel shackled? Are you walking a path of your own choosing? You may want to note down your reactions to these and future questions, but use the time principally for quiet reflection. Paste the feet and legs onto the card near the bottom.

Next, find the piece with the lower body on it and light the next candle. How does your own abdomen feel, relaxed or knotted with anxiety? The stomach is traditionally thought of as the seat of courage and will-power. Is yours strong? Do you trust your gut feelings? Reflect for a while then add this piece to the legs and feet.

Pick up the piece with the heart and light another candle. Are you light-hearted or merely half-hearted? Are you open-hearted? Is your heart in your work or is it elsewhere? Reflect, then add this piece to the others, gradually rebuilding a complete human being.

Find the piece with the throat and mouth on it. Light a candle and think about your workplace. Do you communicate clearly there? Can you speak out? Do you have a voice? Can you express yourself? Consider for a while, then add this piece to the picture too.

Take the piece showing rest of the head and light the next candle. How is your own head? How does your mind feel? You have a brain, eyes and ears. Do you know your own mind? Or are you being brainwashed? Are you open-minded? Are you clear-sighted or do you feel hampered by short-sighted policies? Do you have your own vision? Are you visible? Reflect for a few minutes then add this piece to your nearly completed figure.

Finally, pick up the piece (or pieces) showing the hands and arms. Light the last candle. How do your own hands and arms usually feel? Are you open-handed or tight-fisted? Do you have a free hand and a light touch, or are your hands tied? Can you mould your own future, carve out your own niche? Do you need more elbow room? Can you shoulder your responsibilities? Think about it before adding this last piece to the figure.

Draw around the outline of the body with the gold marker pen, unifying and integrating all the parts. If certain areas have particular issues for you, colour them in with the gold pen. If you feel your voice isn't heard, for example, colour the mouth gold.

Snuff the candles and put the figure where you will see it.

First aid

Take time at odd moments during the day to reconnect with yourself. How are you feeling? If you could do with a little re-balancing, try a ritual for fine-tuning.

Sometimes you just have to give yourself time out. The next

time everything is threatening to get on top of you, make your excuses and take yourself off somewhere quiet. Use a few minutes' breathing space for some ritual visualisation, such as described below.

Anger

You've tried taking a deep breath and counting to ten but you're still seething. Before you explode, use that anger to fuel a harmless visualisation. Imagine a volcano erupting deep inside you. Picture white-hot burning lava spewing out, incandescent embers shooting high into the sky. Touch your forehead and continue to watch as the eruption transforms into a blaze of fireworks, filling the scene with sparkling and shimmering colours. Let your firework display die down then go back to work with a cooler, clearer head.

If pressure builds up again, touch your forehead for a moment and let it discharge in a burst of coloured stars.

Stress

Press your forefingers lightly to your temples. Think of the situation, person or problem that is stressing you. Picture it clearly then watch as a soft, pink mist gradually settles over the scene. Let the mist thicken until it's a pink fog obscuring your view entirely. Shrink the pink until it's just a dot then let it disappear altogether.

Whenever stress threatens, lightly touch your temples again for a moment.

Fear

When you're feeling vulnerable, you need a protective shield. Rest your fingertips lightly together in front of your chest and imagine a bright white light deep inside your heart. As you breathe, picture the light expanding until it envelops you completely in a radiant bubble. Let the bubble solidify into a dazzling reflective surface. Feel secure and at ease in your bubble of light, knowing anything negative will just bounce right off it.

When you need to feel safe, just bring your fingertips lightly together in front of you.

Tiredness

Turn your palms upwards. Imagine standing under a shower. Instead of water, though, a rainbow of light streams over you. Immerse yourself thoroughly in the glorious colours, sensing them washing away all your tiredness and negativity and replacing them with energy and delight.

When you need to refresh, turn your palms upwards again to receive more of that radiant energy.

Challenges, problems and opportunities

Have you noticed how people love telling you problems are just opportunities in disguise? Especially when you have all the problems and they seem to get all the opportunities. Still, there's no use ducking issues. With a little help from rituals you can plot a path through the potholes and minefields of work and gain help and support to face up to challenges, overcome obstacles and seek out opportunities.

Elemental minimiser

Overcoming obstacles is much easier when your mind is tuned to the problem and you feel positive and energised about it. See if the following ritual can put you in a more constructive frame of mind.

YOU WILL NEED:

Paper

Pen with non-waterproof ink

Bowl of water

Fireproof container

Window box, flower pot or garden

Candle

This ritual needs to be done over two evenings, but it does let the four elements get to work on your problem. Light the candle and write down the nature of your setback. Underline it firmly, saying 'this shall be no more'.

First, let water dissolve it. Float the paper in the bowl of water until as much ink as possible has been washed out.

Next, let air purify it. Pin the paper in a secure place outside where it will be in full light and leave it there for the next day.

Then, let fire consume it. Next evening, relight the candle and, taking proper precautions, set light to the dry paper and let it burn to ash.

Finally, let earth conceal it. Take the ashes and bury them in the ground. A window box or planter will do at a pinch.

Shower power

Salt and rain are usually easy to come by, so seize the opportunity for this ritual when it arises.

YOU WILL NEED:

Salt

A paved area outside

A rainy day

Wait until there's a lull in the rain, then go outside and use the salt to mark out a square big enough to stand in. Stand inside it as the rain starts again and watch your obstruction just dissolve away.

Melting moments

Rituals don't come any easier than this one.

YOU WILL NEED:

A red candle

A pin or something similar

Inscribe the rune Isa | near the top of the candle. This rune represents an icicle and signifies things frozen to a standstill. Light the candle and concentrate on obstacles melting away as your ice barrier gradually thaws.

Finding solutions

Finding solutions requires an open mind. Answers to problems can come from deep within your unconscious, but not when it's fogged with doubt and uncertainty. Use the following rituals to clear away misgivings and rekindle your optimism that there will be a positive outcome.

Becoming clear

YOU WILL NEED:

Paper

Brush or pen

Lemon juice

Candle

Light the candle. With the lemon juice, draw a symbol of hope on the paper – maybe a sun, a flower, a bird, an angel or some more specific symbol of the solution you require.

The paper will appear to be blank. Meditate on it for a little while, drawing parallels with the apparent blankness of your situation. Remind yourself 'the answer is there'.

Hold the paper to the warmth of the candle flame, avoiding setting it alight of course, and watch the solution to your problem appear. Believe the answer will develop from your unconscious mind in the same way.

Put the paper where you will see it often.

Unravelling

Long piece of thick wool or yarn

Incense

Piece of music you enjoy

Light the incense and pass the wool through the smoke to energise and bless it. Think about your problem and begin to knot the thread, imagining tying all your frustration into it. Don't tie it too tightly, but continue knotting until the wool is all one big knot.

Hold the knot in your hands for a few moments, saying to yourself 'what has been done can be undone; what is tangled can be smoothed'.

Put the music on, breathe in the incense and, slowly and painstakingly, begin to untie the knots. Take your time and enjoy the music while you do it. With each knot, imagine another part of the problem being resolved.

When you've finished, wind the thread into a neat ball and put it somewhere you'll see it. Play the music once every day until your problem is solved.

Amazing

YOU WILL NEED:

Puzzle book with a maze in it

Pen or pencil

This is a good one for doing unobtrusively at your desk or during a break. Take a couple of deep breaths to focus your mind. Concentrate on your problem, knowing there is a solution to it somewhere.

Continue to concentrate as you work your way through the maze. Imagine looking down on your problem like this, seeing all the possible paths and pitfalls and able to find the way through. Visualise the problem straightening out along with the puzzle – you may take the odd wrong turning but eventually you will reach your goal.

Welcome in

Opportunities favour an open mind, especially one that's tuned to looking out for them.

YOU WILL NEED:

A key – the more ornate and special the better

Bowl of water

Business card or other symbol of your work

A door – at work if possible, at home if not

Work by candlelight if possible. Close the door. Put the key and the business card or symbol into the water. Hold the bowl in your hands and visualise power flowing out of both of them and energising the water. Dip your finger in the water and 'draw' around the doorframe – keep dipping as you go – and over the door handle.

Sit for a while and visualise the handle turning, the door opening and all manner of wonderful things flowing in through it. Hold the key and card in your hand as you imagine. Open the door for real before you leave. Put the key on your key ring. Dry the card and put it in your bag or wallet.

Window of opportunity

Another opportunity to encourage opportunities.

YOU WILL NEED:

A sunny window

Bell

Gold ribbon

Business card or other symbol of your work

Vase of yellow flowers

Put the vase of flowers on the windowsill and open the window wide to let the sunshine in. Ring the bell to alert your unconscious. Wrap the gold ribbon around your business card and tuck it amongst the flower petals. Spend some time at the open window enjoying the flowers and visualising opportunities from far and wide streaming in.

Leave the card and flowers in the sun all day (with the window open if possible). Next day, take the flowers with you to work and put them in a window there. Keep the card, wrapped in the ribbon, in a pocket or wallet.

Creating confidence

When you have confidence you can achieve almost anything you want to. Confidence can help you weather any storm and feel equal to any task. It helps you say yes to the things you want and no the things you don't want. Encourage your self-assurance with one of the following.

Ring of confidence

This ritual brings all four elements to your aid.

YOU WILL NEED:

Red candle

Incense

Stone or pebble

Bowl of water

A ring

Pick up the ring and lay the rest of the things out in front of you. Light the candle. Hold the ring up to the candle and imagine all the passion and energy of fire being drawn into it.

Take your time and let the feeling pass through the ring, up your arm and right into the heart of you.

Next, pass the ring through the incense and visualise the cool grace of air entering it. Again, breathe in the incense and draw the feeling deep into your body and your mind.

Next, touch the ring to the stone and imagine the strength and endurance of the earth passing into it and from there into your body. Feel yourself becoming strong – absolutely rock solid.

Finally, dip the ring in the water and feel the immense power of the sea enter it. Sense the tides within you becoming stronger, washing away all negativity.

Put the ring on your finger and visualise the force of all four elements working in harmony within you. Wear the ring when you need elemental energy.

Sparkler

Did you get gold stars at school? Well now you can award yourself as many as you like.

YOU WILL NEED:

Packet of gold stars

Piece of card

A candle

Light the candle. Spread the stars out in front of you, turning them shiny side up. Gaze at them and imagine yourself at your sparkling best. Every time you think of one of your good points or something you've achieved, stick a star on the card. Stick them at random or make a pattern, whatever you want. The aim is to cover the card with stars. Ransack your memory for every last glittering detail.

Put the card where you will see it and take some stars to work with you to stick up around your workplace.

The charm chair

Become your own confident self.

YOU WILL NEED:

An upright chair

Candles – enough to make a semi-circle around the chair. Night-lights in holders would be ideal

A confidence charm – something you can slip on a ribbon or chain and wear around your neck

Arrange the candles around the chair and light them. Sit opposite the chair and imagine an ideal, poised, charming and confident version of you is sitting on it. Visualise yourself clearly. Talk to this idealised self; find out what they think, how they feel, how they see the world and how they deal with things.

When you feel ready, go and sit in the chair yourself. (Watch out for candles and trailing hems.) Imagine slipping into this confident self's skin. How does it feel? How do you feel? Put your confidence charm around your neck to tie the feeling in. Continue to enjoy it for as long as you like. Visualise yourself being pleasantly confident and genial in a variety of situations.

Wear the charm to remind you of your confident and charming self.

A nice place to work

Yes, you can turn your workplace into a supportive, uplifting environment. Empowerment is only a desktop away.

Tokens, totems and charms can all be used positively to get you up to speed with everyday challenges and even deliver first aid when the unexpected hits. Your workstation can be a special place that radiates a unique energy that empowers you. Perhaps no one else would notice anything unusual, but you will perceive the harmony and energy around you and your desk.

Desk top

Clear away the clutter on your desk. Get rid of rubbish, file papers, make room in a drawer for pens, paperclips, disks, diaries, and such like.

Fill the new-found space with things that make you feel good. Photographs of allies – your family and friends – will remind you of those who give you emotional support. Pictures of you doing things you enjoy will raise your spirits.

A vase of fresh flowers will bring scent and colour into your life. Find room, too, for one or two special things that will help enhance your positive beliefs. Only you will know their symbolic significance.

Blooming success

Careers take time to grow at their own natural pace and they need to be nurtured. Here's a living reminder.

YOU WILL NEED:

Compost-filled flower pot

Seeds – windowsill herbs such as basil are good for this, but use any easily grown plant

Paper and pen

Candle

Light the candle. Write your name and position or job title on the paper. Underneath, write 'as these seeds grow and prosper, so shall my success'. Bury the paper deep in the compost. Plant the seeds on top, following the instructions on the packet.

Water the seeds and tend the young seedlings as they appear. Put the pot on your desk or windowsill and nurture the plants well, watering, feeding and checking them regularly. As they flourish, so should your fortunes.

The animal in you

Totem animals have long been used to remind people of different strengths and qualities.

YOU WILL NEED:

A candle

A figure or picture of the animal of your choice. Pick an animal that embodies traits that would be helpful to you in your job, such as one of those listed below

- EAGLE – a high-flyer with the gift of far-sightedness
- HORSE – swift and powerful with stamina and grace
- BULL – a protector of others with strength and determination
- FOX – playful and cunning
- CAT – patience and concentration; subtlety and grace
- BEAR – honest and unpretentious, powerful in defence
- WOLF – fiercely independent yet loyal and true to the pack
- OWL – the wise one who sees what is hidden
- DOLPHIN – a free and playful spirit with understanding and awareness

Light the candle. Hold your totem in your hands and imagine the spirit of the animal. Visualise yourself becoming one with it, immerse yourself in the sights, sounds and sensations as you run, fly or swim together. Let the strength of the animal become yours.

Take the figure or picture to work and put it on your desk as a daily reminder. When you need to make a decision or take action, pause for a moment and reflect on your totem animal.

Desk drawer

Keep a spiritual first aid kit in your drawer to keep you on form and fighting fit. Include any or all of the following items.

CARDS

- SPIRIT CARDS – see *Pick a card*, page 25
- COLOUR CARDS – see *Pick a colour*, page 27

Pick a card and spend a few moments breathing slowly and quietly just gazing at it, letting the quality or colour simply wash through you. Prop it up somewhere where you can continue to glance at it as and when you want.

- DECISION CARDS – see *Decisions, decisions*, page 33

Keep these by you for instant decision-making advice.

ELEMENTS

Find four small pictures that represent the four elements. Picture postcards would be ideal, but photos or illustrations cut from magazines would do perfectly well.

- EARTH – picture of forest, meadows or similar
- WATER – picture of sea, lake or stream
- FIRE – picture of flames, volcano, etc
- AIR – picture of clouds, birds or butterflies

Choose a picture that evokes the feeling you need. Visualise the power of that element surging through your body.

- EARTH – nurturing and empowering. Imagine strong roots growing deep into the ground connecting you to the power of life

- WATER – cleansing and healing. Visualise it flowing over and through you, washing away all negativity

- FIRE – energy. Feel yourself becoming energised and alive

- AIR – inspiration. Imagine a cool, fresh breeze blowing all your mental cobwebs away

ESCAPE PICTURES

- ESCAPE PICTURES – see *Picture peace*, page 38

Gaze at your chosen picture for a few minutes and escape the humdrum world on a well-deserved soul holiday.

MOTIVATOR

What are you working for? What motivates you? Your children's future, smiling satisfied clients or customers, a new car, world travel, promotion? Keep an object or a picture that represents it in your desk to remind you when you wonder if it's all worth it.

The little book of success

Make a little book of your successes as an instant antidote to low self-esteem.

YOU WILL NEED:

A beautiful notebook

In your notebook list absolutely everything you are or have ever been successful at. Write down all your lifetime's achievements going right back as far as you can remember and including even the tiniest things – the big ones get a whole page to themselves. Use gold ink and colour to underline and decorate the pages. Stick stars and coloured transfers on if you want. Keep the book in your drawer for when your confidence and self-esteem need a boost.

Chapter Nine
The Enchanted Year

Seasons of the soul

Connecting to the enchantment of everyday life also awakens your awareness of the deeper rhythms of existence. The sun has its great yearly cycle, moving from the dead of winter through to the abundance of harvest time. The moon has its own phases, waxing and waning with the months. Life too has cycles, and rituals harmonise the emotional and spiritual needs of these times.

These days, our personal calendars tend to revolve more around the school year or the tax year than around the old cycles of sowing and reaping, but try some of these rituals to keep the old sense of a stately progression through the seasons. They aim to help you maintain a natural order of events that will help keep your inner world and the natural world in harmony with each other.

The Lunar Calendar

The waxing and waning of the moon as it goes through its monthly cycle has long been of symbolic significance. Harness a little moon power by planning your activities according to the lunar calendar.

Waxing and full

The new moon represents new opportunities. The new moon has its horns facing left, like a backward 'C'. It symbolises growth and potential and it's a good time to start anything you want to see grow and prosper. Start something new or put plans into action any time between the new moon and the full, but the earlier the better. Get them off to a good start with this ritual.

YOU WILL NEED:

White candle

A silver charm or a piece of silver jewellery

Paper and pen

Plant pot and packet of seeds – white flowers would be nice or a silver-leafed herb

Sit where you can see the new moon and light the candle. By its clear, calm light, sit and think about your new plan or project. Write down what you intend to do and what you want to happen. Fold the paper as small as you can and bury it in the plant pot. Sow the seeds on top.

Hold the silver charm up to the moon and visualise all the potential of the new moon pouring into it. In a few days, the moon will ripen from a thin sliver to a silver globe. Your plans have the potential to ripen and come to fruition in the same natural way.

Keep the charm with you to remind you of your plans. Water and tend the seeds as they take root and develop. Tend your plans likewise, giving them a little attention every day as they, too, germinate and grow.

Waning and dark

The old moon is a time for endings. The horns of the old, waning moon point to the right, like a 'C'. It symbolises reduction and decline and it's a good time to do a ritual for anything you want to see decrease and grow less. When you want to shake off a bad habit, drop an addiction or go on a diet, make a start any time after the full moon. Let the symbolism of that dwindling disc aid your will-power.

YOU WILL NEED:

White candle

A silver charm or a piece of silver jewellery

Paper and pen

Fireproof container

Sit where you will see the moon – the older it is the later it rises, so be prepared for some after-midnight work if you pick a moon much past the full. Light the candle and sit and think about what you want to get rid of in your life. Write down how you feel about it, how it has hurt you or held you back in the past. On another sheet, write down what you want to happen instead and what you intend to do about it. Fold the first paper and hold it in the flame of the candle. Let it burn away to ash in the fireproof container.

Hold the silver charm up to the moon and visualise the power of the old moon flowing into it. In a few days, that moon will dwindle from a silver globe, to a slender splinter, to absolutely nothing. Whatever you feel has a hold over you will dwindle and diminish in exactly the same way.

Wrap the second paper, the one with your new intentions on it, around the charm. Keep them safe and at the next new moon use them to do the waxing moon ritual explained above.

The Solar Calendar

Every culture and people has its seasonal round of festivities and celebrations. The ancient Celts kept both a solar and a lunar calendar that gave them a cycle of light and dark, birth and death, summer and winter.

The solar calendar describes the journey of the sun from the darkness of winter, through to its full glory at midsummer and back into darkness again. It is essentially a rural calendar, following the seasons with the cycle of ploughing, sowing and reaping.

There is something deep in our unconscious minds that also follows this cycle of the seasons, summer and winter, light and dark, seedtime and harvest. Few of us now live in a rural environment, though, dependent on the date of celebrations to know when to plant corn or harvest hay. But we can still harness this deep impulse in order to harmonise our own internal cycles and live with our natural rhythms rather than in spite of them.

Each of the following old solar festivals includes suggestions for an altar, a theme for the day and a ritual to help you get into the mood to celebrate it accordingly.

Yule and the winter solstice

The winter solstice, the old festival of Yule, comes a few days before Christmas on 21 December. It's the shortest day, the day before the sun begins its long, slow climb back to summer. Think of it as the opening of the Christmas celebrations that celebrate the sun's (or Son's) rebirth.

It's traditionally a time for completion, the closing of one year and the beginning of the next. Get ready for the new year by completing as much unfinished business and tying up as many loose ends as you can. Complete those odd jobs that have been hanging around; get your correspondence and filing in order. Have a clear-out and get rid of those things you've finished with. Make sure your life – physically and metaphorically – is as clear and uncluttered as you can make it. The more clutter you clear out, the more room you have to invite good things into your life.

ALTAR

The winter solstice celebrates the change from shortening days to lengthening ones. It's the promise that, even at the darkest heart of winter, spring and summer will come and the sun will return.

Make a candle altar to reflect this. Collect together a variety of candles, especially red, orange and gold ones, in all the shapes and sizes you can find. Add lots of gold, mirrors, and any other bright, shiny things that will reflect the light.

Among the candles tuck slips of paper bearing your thanks for the achievements of the year just gone and your hopes and ambitions for the year to come. (Remember, though, to keep fire safety in mind.)

This altar will also be very useful for the solstice ritual given below.

THE THEME OF THE DAY IS ...

Clear out your bodily clutter. Symbolic or not, you might be glad you had a day lightly fasting when you get to the Christmas festivities.

Eat lots of yellow- and orange-coloured food to celebrate the sun and help clear out your system. Oranges, lemon juice, russet apples, carrots, pumpkin and squash – make soups and juices throughout the day. Drink hot water with lemon juice, and ginger tea sweetened with golden honey. Hold juices up to whatever sunlight there might be and visualise them becoming energised.

Make the most of what light there is by going for a brisk morning or lunchtime walk or cycle ride. Stop for a moment where you can see trees or bushes to sense the life in everything deeply withdrawn into itself. Not fretting or worrying about what it should be doing, just resting and waiting for the first touch of the sun to awaken it and start everything blossoming into life again.

Prepare a *Soul Bath* (see page 41), and add orange and lemon oils. Bathe by candlelight and visualise the light and scent flowing into you. Breathe it deeply in and imagine it filling you with a warm radiance.

Winter solstice ritual

If you've made a solstice candle altar, use it for this ritual. If not, use half a dozen or so white or gold candles.

YOU WILL NEED:

Altar or candles, as above

Pen and paper

Candle snuffer, if you can get hold of one

Matches or lighter

Light all the candles on your altar or wherever you are performing the ritual. Sit and think about the year that has passed. Think about what's important to you – work, relationships, spiritual or creative growth, or a specific goal or ambition. Take time to make a real, uncritical assessment – what went well; what you would do differently another time; what you've achieved; what you can leave behind and what you want to take forward. Write down the key points on a piece of paper. Fold it ready to put away safely in a diary, keepsake book, or wherever you keep things like that.

Either with the candle snuffer or with your thumb and finger, snuff out all the candle flames. Sit for a while in the darkness. This is the gap between the year that has gone and the one that is coming; a moment's pause before the whole great cycle starts again. For the moment there's nothing; the past has gone and the future is yet to come.

Cast your mind back to the trees and bushes and the life withdrawn deeply inside them, resting and waiting. Say goodbye to the past and let your deepest hopes for the future arise within you out of the darkness.

Take the matches or lighter and re-light the candles. Take a minute to welcome the light and warmth back into your life. The sun has returned and the new cycle has begun. Think about your hopes and plans for the coming year. Write down your key goals and intentions. Fold the paper and either put it on the altar or put it underneath one of the candles. Leave the candles to burn for a while.

Spring equinox

The spring equinox falls on 21 March. It's a time when the day and night are of equal length. After the equinox, every day becomes longer until midsummer and the longest day. The spring equinox is traditionally a time for renewal. With lighter evenings, warmer days and the flowers and trees in bud, it's really spring at last. It's Easter-tide, and Easter Day itself can fall at any time between now and the end of April, or thereabouts.

This is the first flowering. Look at your hopes and plans for the year – some of them should be coming into flower now, if not quite yet bearing fruit. If they're not, warm them with a little of your energy and attention.

Cultivate your seedling plans. Weed out problems now before they get too big. Feed and water every day with your care and interest. Note what could do with some 'fertiliser' in the form of a time or money investment. Is there new ground that needs breaking before you sow seeds of hope?

ALTAR

This is very much a flower festival. Spring flowers should be abundant now, so decorate your altar with them. Add light green, lilac and yellow candles for the colours of spring. Eggs are traditional as a symbol of new life – put a basket of coloured eggs on the altar and lay your wishes on slips of paper in with them. A bowl of spring rainwater is a nice touch, too.

THE THEME OF THE DAY IS ...

Energy. As the world blossoms, so could you. Start the day with a *Power Shower* (see page 23). Start with a brisk dry-brush body massage to stimulate your circulation, and finish with a blast of cold water.

Eat lots of live foods throughout the day to celebrate new life and help stimulate the life force within you. Try raw fruits and vegetables in salads or juices, sprouting beans and seeds, live yoghurt with active bio-cultures. Drink fresh juice and lots of spring water. Hold them up to the sun and visualise energy pouring into them.

Get out into the world by taking a brisk morning or lunchtime walk or cycle ride. Go where you can see flowers and hear birds – a park or garden, or out into the countryside if possible. Stop for a moment to sense the life in everything. Feel it budding and bursting effortlessly and abundantly.

In the evening, prepare a *Soul Bath* (see page 41) and add spring flower petals to the bundle. Bathe by candlelight and visualise the light and energy from the flowers flowing into you. Breathe it deeply in and imagine it filling you with the clarity, energy and radiance of spring.

Spring equinox ritual

Let your life blossom with the season.

YOU WILL NEED:

Light green candles – as many as you like

Pen and paper

Plant pot and seed compost

Packet of seeds

Light the candles. Write your name on the paper; fold it and hold it in your hands. In the clear, calm candlelight, sit and think about your own life and the new life happening all around you. Think back to that quiet moment with the flowers and the birds, sensing the effortless, budding, bursting abundance.

Close your eyes and visualise yourself as a caterpillar. Imagine slowly turning into a chrysalis before breaking out of that tight casing to become a butterfly. Stretch your wings and feel the warm sun on them. Try your wings out and understand you can overcome any hurdles or obstacles.

Bury the paper with your name on it in the plant pot and sow the seeds on top. As the plants blossom, so will you, naturally and easily.

Summer solstice

The summer solstice falls on 21 June. This is midsummer, the longest day, and from here on the sun will decline and the days start to grow shorter although summer itself will continue to blaze on.

Traditionally, it's a time when the veil between the worlds is said to be at its thinnest. This is an especially magical time for dreaming and imagining. Summer is at its height, and everything is still lush and green before the heat and dust of late summer. With the seeds sown and growing well, this was customarily a chance for a brief respite to play and dream a little before the fruits ripened and the harvest began.

Take the time to dream. Who are you? What are your deepest wishes and desires?

ALTAR

This is an altar for abundance. Decorate it with your richest things. Add the summer flowers that are now at their height – especially richly scented roses. Burn lots of gold and silver candles.

Count your blessings, write them down and place them, with thanks, on the altar. Give special thanks for all that is now in full flower in your life. Include any 'otherworld' symbols you might have – fairies are especially representative of this time of the year.

THE THEME OF THE DAY IS …

Relaxation. Relax your body and open your mind to dreams. Constant 'busyness' absorbs the attention at a shallow level to the exclusion of our deeper instincts and intuition.

Make a serene start to the day with calming music while you dress and have breakfast. Take time for twenty or thirty minutes of meditation or gentle stretching exercises to music early on in the morning. Throughout the day, take regular breaks of five minutes or so just to relax and let go completely, with deep breaths, letting all the tension out of your body.

Eat lightly throughout the day and include lots of green herbs and salads in your meals. Flower-petal salads with nasturtiums and marigolds are perfect for today. Pour boiling water over a generous teaspoon of rose petals and sweeten with honey to make rose petal tea.

Take a late evening walk to enjoy the sun. Watch the long shadows striding beside you or in front of you as you walk. Go up somewhere high, if you can, to absorb the full power of the sun.

Take a luxurious *Soul Bath* (see page 41) with rose and other scented flower petals. Play soothing music and bathe by candlelight. Visualise the soft light from the candles mingling with the flower scent and breathe it deeply in. Imagine it filling you with soft radiance.

Summer solstice ritual

The dream world is a place where anything can happen, a world of limitless possibilities. Attune to your own inner dreams with this ritual.

YOU WILL NEED:

Two white or silver candles

Cushions or something similar so you can lie comfortably and relax

Light the candles. Sit or lie comfortably and take a few deep, calm breaths. Focus on a recent, pleasant dream you have had, maybe one that has puzzled you or stayed with you.

Call up the images you remember and visualise yourself back in the dream. When you are there, begin to question the characters and even the objects involved: 'Who are you? What do you want? Why are you in my dream? What do you want to tell me?' These are all good places to start. Accept the first answer that comes into your mind, although you may have to wait patiently for a response. If a character walks away, follow them and let them lead you deeper into the dream.

The various characters and objects in dreams represent aspects of our own character – sometimes our hidden potential, sometimes our darker side. By allowing them to have their say, you discover which parts of yourself want to communicate with you and the message they want to deliver.

Don't try to 'interpret' your dream. Although people may share common symbols, on the whole each dream is unique to the dreamer. If you simply question your dream in the way described above you will arrive at an exclusive message, just for you, from the deepest part of yourself.

Bring yourself back to your full waking state and, if you like, jot down a few notes about what you have discovered.

You may decide, after this ritual, you want to keep a dream diary. Dedicate a special book just for your dreams. Keep it by your bed and note down the key images you remember when you wake up. Re-enter the dream and question at your leisure.

Autumn equinox

On 21 September the days and nights are again of equal length, but from now the days will get shorter and the nights longer. The Earth is going down into darkness and winter again in the great cycle of the seasons.

This is the harvest time. Review your hopes and plans – they should be beginning to bear fruit. If they're not, see if a little 'fertiliser' in the form of time or money will bring them along.

Begin to reap your rewards and celebrate your successes. Protect any tender, undeveloped ideas from the cold winter winds of impatience or disillusionment, but cut out the dead wood. Sort through your harvest and find the seeds of next year's hopes and dreams.

ALTAR

This is an altar of fruition. Decorate it with fruits and autumn flowers. If the leaves have started to turn, include some of their copper and golden glory as well. Burn deep yellow, orange and red candles.

Write out your successes and put them on the altar for you to read and enjoy. Celebrate them unreservedly.

THE THEME OF THE DAY IS ...

Positivity and balance. Autumn can be a rather poignant time. Keep your spirits up with a day dedicated to harmony and wellbeing.

Welcome the day with a *Wake up and breathe* ritual (see page 21). Follow it up with *Open to the day* (see page 20) and welcome in the fruits of autumn. Make time early on in the morning for twenty or thirty minutes of gentle stretching exercises to the sort of music that lifts your spirits. As you stretch, feel your body becoming more balanced and receptive.

Eat harvest foods today. Wholegrains and cereals, apples, nuts and seeds. Add warming spices such as ginger, cinnamon and nutmeg. Drink rosehip and bramble teas – teas from hedgerow fruits to remind you of the bounty of autumn.

If the first frost has happened, the trees may just be beginning to turn about now. Take a walk or cycle ride in woodland, park or garden to enjoy the sun and the gold reflected in the leaves. If possible, go somewhere you find particularly beautiful.

Prepare a *Soul Bath* (see page 41) with ginger, cinnamon and nutmeg, and any other aromatic spices you like. Light candles and visualise their soft light blending with the warm, spicy fragrance. Breathe it in, drawing it deeply into you. Imagine it filling you with the soft, golden light of the autumn sun.

Autumn equinox ritual

Find a power animal – an animal totem – to take with you into the winter with this ritual.

YOU WILL NEED:

Two deep orange candles

Light the candles, breathe deeply and relax. Close your eyes and imagine walking through an autumn wood. Follow the path ahead of you until you find yourself in a clearing. Sit and wait and your animal ally will come to you. When it does, welcome it warmly and pat it or stroke it. Visualise becoming one with the animal. Take time to absorb its energy and feel its power. Become aware of its character, its wisdom and its physical strengths within you. Take some time to simply enjoy being one with this animal. Share its running, flying, swimming, hunting, grooming, grazing or whatever else you like.

Come back into your own body. Thank your power animal and tell it how glad you are it came to you and how much you look forward to meeting it again in the future.

Back in the waking world, find a small charm, picture or figure to represent your power animal and remind you of its strengths. Think how these strengths could help you and aim to develop them in yourself. Go back and visit whenever you like, and call on your power animal whenever you need to access its particular qualities.

Festivals

As well as the solar year, the ancient Celts also celebrated four great festivals at the four quarters of the year. These were times of great feasting and celebration, often lasting a full three days. Some are still kept, in one way or another, but the following rituals try to interpret them usefully in ways meaningful to us today in the modern world while still keeping those connections to ancient tradition.

As above, each has an altar, a theme for the day and a ritual to help you get into the mood of the day and celebrate it accordingly.

Imbolc

Imbolc, or Candlemas, falls on 2 February. This is a festival of faith and hope. Just when everything seems dead, deep underground new life is stirring, and the first signs are just now becoming visible. It's about the justification of faith and keeping optimism alive when everything seemed hopeless. It is a quiet, reflective time, underpinned with a quiet joy at the return of light and life to the world.

Celebrate Imbolc to renew your trust in the world and welcome the light into your heart.

ALTAR

Make a quiet, reflective, simple altar to reflect the season. Use a white cloth, and include dozens of tiny candles or night-lights in silver or white to symbolise the first return of light to the world. If you can find early spring flowers such as crocuses or snowdrops, add these as well. If you like, scatter silver stars over the altar to reflect tiny points of light.

Write your hopes and dreams on little pieces of paper and slip them in among the candles. Bury them in the newly stirring earth with thanks after you've dismantled the altar.

THE THEME OF THE DAY IS ...

Purification. Cleanse your mind and body ready to absorb the coming spring. Start the day with a glass of hot water and lemon juice, and continue to drink hot water at regular intervals throughout the day to cleanse your system. Spend twenty or thirty minutes in meditation or gentle stretching exercises. Take regular breaks of five minutes or so throughout the day to visualise breathing life and light in, and darkness and toxins out.

Eat light-coloured foods today – rice, white fish or chicken, pale fruits and vegetables, natural yoghurt. Flavour with vanilla or lemon. If you eat by candlelight, hold food and drink up to the light and visualise energy flowing into it from the flame.

Go for a morning or lunchtime walk or cycle ride and look for the small signs of awakening life – the first shoots breaking the ground, a bird singing, a sign of buds beginning to form.

In the afternoon or evening, take a purifying bath. Add a handful of salt to the water, light candles around the bath and relax. Visualise the salt gently drawing toxins out through your skin. Inhale and, as you breathe out, visualise blockages, debris and toxins being flushed right out of your body. Draw your breath deeply into your brain and picture dark thoughts and memories being flushed out of there, too, leaving you clear and clean.

Imbolc ritual

As the ice melts in the real world, melt any lingering ice in your heart or soul with this ritual.

YOU WILL NEED:

A white candle and something to engrave it with

A bowl of ice cubes – if it's icy or snowing outside, use the natural thing

A bowl of potted spring flowers – narcissi, hyacinth or crocuses, for example – preferably still in bud and about to flower

Inscribe the candle with the rune Isa, $|$, which symbolises an icicle. Light the candle and sit comfortably and quietly while the flame burns down through the rune and the ice melts. As it does, visualise all the coldness and darkness of winter melting away from you. Visualise, too, any coldness or stiffness in your heart or soul just melting and flowing away. Picture any coldness in your life melting like snow at the touch of the sun. Sense new life flowing into you, awakening the hope and faith deep inside you. Send beams of light to all the people you know.

When the ice has melted, pour it onto the bowl of flowers to water them. Tend them and watch them bloom.

Beltane

Also honoured as May Day, 1 May is the day spring turns into summer. It's a life-affirming celebration of beauty, youth and life with its May Queens, May blossom and maypoles, and dancing and feasting to ensure the continued fertility of the Earth.

Celebrate Beltane to draw out the youthful, beautiful part of yourself, physically, emotionally and spiritually, and ensure the continued blossoming of your heart, mind and soul.

ALTAR

Make your altar as beautiful as you possibly can for this festival. Use gorgeous fabric for the altar cloth and bring out your finest flower bowls and candle holders. This is, traditionally, the one day of the year you can bring May blossom (hawthorn) inside without ill luck befalling you, so make the most of it. Smother the altar in flowers of all types and colours, especially the scented ones. Burn lots of incense, especially the flowery types such as amber and rose.

Include affirmations about beauty and self-worth. Sit before your altar and absorb the beauty deep into your soul.

THE THEME OF THE DAY IS …

Pleasure and beauty. Pamper your body today and put yourself in a beautiful frame of mind. Today is the day to use all those things you've been keeping for best. Use your finest china and cutlery, eat your favourite foods, surround yourself with flowers, wear your most beautiful clothes and perfumes.

Start the day with a luxury breakfast, whatever you most desire. Eat it while listening to your favourite music and, if possible, looking at a lovely view. If you don't have the view, find some beautiful object or picture to look at. Remember, the object of the day is to drench yourself in beauty.

Go for a walk and search out beauty. When you find it, breathe it deeply into your soul. Use your breath to visualise breathing beauty and life in, and negativity out. Take a few minutes regularly throughout the day to visualise breathing beauty in and negativity out.

Take a picnic lunch of your favourite foods and search out a bower to eat it in. Enjoy the scents, sights and sounds of nature as you eat. Take the afternoon off to do something you really enjoy or simply be with friends.

In the evening, enjoy a luxurious *Soul Bath* (see page 41) and add May blossom and other scented flower petals to the mix. Add your favourite essential oils too. Play beautiful music and bathe by candlelight. Visualise the soft light from the candles mingling with the flowery scent and breathe it deeply in. Imagine it filling you with flowers.

Beltane ritual

Get to know your higher self – the joyful, wise, loving, creative, unfettered part of you – through this ritual.

YOU WILL NEED:

Two silver candles

Pen and paper

Light the candles, breathe deeply and relax. Close your eyes and imagine walking through a May-day garden, filled with blossom and birdsong. Feel the sun warm against your skin as you follow the path until you come to a bridge over a river. Cross the bridge and climb some steps up to a small summer-house. Sit and wait and ask your higher self to come to you.

When they arrive, welcome them warmly. Talk to them, ask any questions you have and receive the answers with understanding and acceptance. Take time getting to know this higher part of you. Become aware of their character, wisdom and strengths, and how they reveal themself within you. Take some time to enjoy simply being with this remarkable aspect of yourself. Finally, ask them to show you a word or a symbol from your deepest unconscious mind that will empower you.

Thank your higher self for this meeting, tell them how glad

you are to know them and how much you look forward to meeting again in the future. Retrace your way back down the steps and over the bridge.

Back in the waking world, draw the symbol or write down the word. Look at it or say it to yourself to remind you of your higher self. Think how the wisdom, love, joy and strength of your higher self could help you, and decide how you will develop them. Go back and visit whenever you like, and call on your higher self whenever you need to access their benign strength.

Lammas

Lammas, 1 August, traditionally celebrates the start of the harvest season and the first grain harvest of the year. Although the sun is still high and the days hot and long, the year is perceptibly moving on and autumn with its bountiful harvest will arrive in due course.

Celebrate Lammas to honour all the good things in your life and ensure continuing fruitfulness for your heart, mind and soul.

ALTAR

Heap the altar with all the things you value in your life – either actually or using symbols, pictures or photographs of them. Include friends, family, pets, things you enjoy doing, places you enjoy going, your talents and abilities, your favourite anything and everything. Make your altar as vivid and joyous as you possibly can. Add the seasonal flowers and fruits of generous August.

Include affirmations about abundance and thank-you notes to everyone who makes your life better. Sit before your altar and celebrate the wealth and richness symbolised there.

This altar will also be very useful if you are doing the ritual suggested below.

THE THEME OF THE DAY IS ...

Abundance and plenty. Put yourself in an expansive frame of mind with an unhurried day and introduce more elbow room into your life.

Try to respect your own natural rhythm of waking, eating and sleeping today. Plan unhurried meals and eat them when you feel hungry rather than because the clock says it's time to.

Start the day with a leisurely bath, followed by an easy-going breakfast. Base your diet around wholegrains and cereals today, if you like, in honour of the grain harvest.

Go for a leisurely walk and observe the sheer abundance of nature, especially when it comes to fruits and seeds. Millions created and released in hope and faith they will flower and bear fruit in their own time. Visualise how this idea could be translated into your own life.

Throughout the day, take a couple of minutes at fairly regular intervals to inhale deeply and stretch. Expand your whole body, filling the space around you. Visualise breathing in abundance – abundant time, abundant space, abundant resources.

Plan a relaxed evening meal. Invite friends over, if you like. The aim of the meal is to feed your soul as well as simply fill your stomach. Set a lavish table with flowers and candles and take your time over the meal, enjoying everything – scent, sight and sound as well as taste. Food eaten with all your senses nourishes your spirit as well as your body.

Last thing in the evening, play beautiful music and bathe by candlelight. Take all the time in the world and go to bed relaxed and serene.

Lammas ritual

Celebrate your own harvest of life with this ritual.

YOU WILL NEED:

> *Your Lammas altar. If you don't have one, gather together fruits and flowers along with photographs and symbols of the important people and things in your life*

> *A photograph of yourself*

> *Two natural honeycomb candles*

> *A deep gold or orange flower – think of the August sun when choosing*

> *Pen and paper*

> *An envelope*

Light the candles. Look at all the good things on your altar, or the things you have gathered together, and think about the richness of life with thanks and celebration.

Take a sheet of paper and write down all the things that have made you happy and all the things you've achieved over the past year. Look at the picture of yourself and congratulate yourself on filling your life with goodness. Thank anyone or anything else you would like to, as well.

Take a second sheet of paper and write down all the things still missing from your life – the things you would like to have, like to be, like to experience or achieve.

Fold the two pieces of paper together and put the golden flower on top. Drink in its colour and vibrancy. Visualise a strong, warm golden light shining around you from the flower. Imagine the two lists melting together in the radiance of it, picture them running together like molten gold and blending with the light. Imagine all the things you have achieved strengthening and supporting all the things you still want to achieve.

See yourself glowing with light, opening to possibilities, your optimism, expectation and determination becoming stronger and brighter. Deep down, you know you can harvest even richer rewards in your life.

Fold the two lists around your photo and put them in the envelope. Put the envelope somewhere safe.

Samhain

Samhain, or Halloween, which begins at sunset on 31 October, is probably the best-known of the ancient festivals. It was the old Celtic New Year and, traditionally, a time of purification and renewal. It celebrates life continuing despite the tightening grip of winter as the year slips into the dark months. Its associations with the Day of the Dead, ghosts, and other symbols of death are clear.

Celebrate Samhain to banish your own ghosts and shadows and remind you of your ancestral inheritance. Generation succeeds generation and life goes on, just as season succeeds season through its cycle of light and dark.

ALTAR

Make an ancestor altar for this festival. Use photographs of your relatives, as far back as they go, and any keepsakes or mementoes of them you may have. Include photographs of your own younger self amongst them as well.

Add things that symbolise the culture or background you come from, and anything you feel symbolises your predecessors. If, for example, they were farmers or fishermen, include something that represents that type of life to you; if they lived in another country, include symbols of that place. If they had strong religious or social beliefs you know about, include these, also.

Include anything old you feel a connection with, whether it

comes from your family or not. The purpose of this altar is to establish a connection to the past, and especially with your own heritage.

Sit quietly before your altar and acknowledge where you fit into all this, what your cultural and emotional inheritance is.

This altar will also be very useful if you are doing the ritual suggested below.

THE THEME OF THE DAY IS ...

Tradition. Find out who you are and where you come from. Put yourself in context. You'll feel stronger with the weight of history behind you supporting you.

Look through family albums; try to work out your family tree, as far as you can. Today is a good day for talking to family members about what you were like as a child. Talk to older family members about what they remember about the family history. If you're not in contact with your family, search out stories and histories about where you live or a place you feel attached too. Find out if there are any local customs or family traditions.

Base your meals today around traditional dishes – either local or regional traditions, or family recipes.

Find out the history of where you live. Local libraries usually have lots of information, often collected by local groups or societies. Go for a walk around your neighbourhood, trying to follow the old paths and imagining what was there before, and how it has changed. Old roads are surprisingly persistent, even new towns are often built on old roads or trackways. Street names give away the history of a place, too.

Alternatively, go to an historic town or ancient site for the day. Whichever you do, try to get a sense of the old places still lying hidden under the new. Observe how the old often provides the bones of the new. Visualise how this idea affects, or could affect, your own life.

Take time throughout the day to stop and experience who and where you are. Stand still, take a few deep, relaxing breaths, feel your feet firmly on the earth, and connect fully to where you are. Take in what you see, hear, feel and smell, and maybe even what you taste. Remind yourself you are right here, right now.

Samhain ritual

Banish your own particular bogeymen with this ritual.

YOU WILL NEED:

> Your ancestor altar, or family photos and artefacts
>
> A photograph of yourself
>
> Two dark-coloured candles
>
> A white candle
>
> Pen and paper
>
> A fireproof container

Light the dark-coloured candles. Look at the family represented on your altar, or in the photos you've collected together. Think about this visible symbol of your long line of descent over thousands of years to be who you are today, right now. Think about your forebears and the richness of your inheritance from them. Think of your origins with thanks and celebration.

With the full support of all the generations who came before you, begin thinking about your own fears and obstacles. Take a sheet of paper and write down all the things you fear and all the things that habitually hold you back.

Take the photo of yourself and put it near the front of the altar, or wherever else you are doing the ritual. Put the white candle in front of it, but don't light it yet. Visualise your fears and doubts as dark shadows crowding around you. See them eclipsing you in your photograph, oppressing and overshadowing you. Then visualise a clear golden light sweeping all those shadows away. Light the white candle so its light falls on your photo. Watch the flame banish the darkness.

Tear your list of fears into tiny pieces. Drop them in the fireproof container and set light to them. Watch as they burn away into ash. Visualise that clear golden light sweeping through your life, chasing away the gloom.

Keep the light burning in front of your photo for a while. Use the time to visualise what your life will be like free of fears and oppression. What is the first thing you want to do? Decide on the first steps to achieving it, however small.

Your birthday

Lastly, a personal festival which should be celebrated every year with great enthusiasm ...

Birthdays are for celebrating *you*. It's nice when friends and relations remember and send cards and gifts, but the person with most to celebrate about your birth is *you*, so make the day special.

ALTAR

Build a special shrine for your birthday each year. As well as cards and gifts, include photos of yourself at various times in your life. It gives a lovely feeling of continuation and a real sense of who you are when you can glance back over your own history. Include, too, things that represent your hopes and dreams for the year ahead.

Give yourself a special present, something you've long wished for but wouldn't normally buy just for you, to affirm your own value to yourself.

THE THEME OF THE DAY IS ...

Pure self-indulgence, of course. Decide beforehand what would make your perfect day and organise everything so all you have to do is enjoy it. If you're stuck for an idea try a day down memory lane.

MORNING – Re-live your childhood. This morning, take all the time you want to play. Either play games or sports – but keep it light-hearted, not competitive – or let those creative urges out. Get organised with paints, paper, clay, beads, ribbons, whatever appeals to you, and express yourself.

Afternoon – Become a teenager again. Remember the energy you had? Put on some music and dance. Spend the afternoon trying on clothes, shopping for accessories, trying out new versions of you. Get your flirting muscles working again. Try a new experience, something you always wanted to do but never got around to. Recapture the feeling you had when everything was new and you could be anything you wanted.

Evening – You're an adult, enjoy all the sophisticated adult things you looked forward to when you were young. Dress in luxurious clothes, wear wonderful fragrances, have dinner in an exotic restaurant and be witty and charming all evening. Do something you always planned to do 'when you were a grown-up'.

Birthday ritual

Everyone makes a wish before they blow their birthday candles out. Make your wish more of an intention with this birthday ritual.

YOU WILL NEED:

A white candle and something to engrave it with

Pick a word that symbolises all you want for the coming year. Love, joy, success, strength, laughter, for example, or it could be something more abstract and personal that has a special meaning for you.

First thing in the morning of your birthday, inscribe this word along with your own name on the white candle. Light the candle and let the flame carry your wishes to the universe on a beam of light. Focus on your intention and make a pledge to yourself to do all you can to help it come true.

Picture yourself sitting by candlelight at the same time next year, reviewing the great time you've had and the satisfaction you had making it all happen. Leave the candle to burn while you visualise, then make a wish and blow it out.

I

Index of Rituals